Alphaeus Hunton:

The Unsung Valiant

Alphaeus Hunton:

The Unsung Valiant

By Dorothy Hunton

Foreword by Charisse Burden-Stelly

ISBN 10: 0-7178-0832-7   ISBN-13 978-07178-0832-8
Typeset by Amnet Systems, Chennai, India

ALPHAEUS HUNTON:
THE UNSUNG VALIANT

CONTENTS

Foreword		vii
Preface		xii
Chronology		xv
1.	The Beginning	1
2.	Howard University	22
3.	Transition	32
4.	The National Negro Congress	46
5.	The Council on African Affairs (Part I)	56
6.	The Council on African Affairs (Part II)	74
7.	Prison: The Bail Fund Affair	81
8.	Broadening Horizons	93
9.	Guinea: A New Career	112
10.	Ghana: The Encyclopedia Africana	128
11.	Shattered Hopes: The Ghanaian Coup	148
12.	Zambia: Last Years	163
References		181
Appendix		183

FOREWORD

On August 8, 1951, the preeminent Pan-Africanist Dr. W.E.B. Du Bois wrote a letter expressing his concern about the arrest of Dr. William Alphaeus Hunton, Jr. During the height of McCarthyism, Hunton had been imprisoned for six months for refusing to turn over the names of persons who had contributed to the Civil Rights Congress's (CRC) bail fund. According to Du Bois, Hunton was a "quiet, studious, conscientious and absolutely incorruptible" man whose only crime was his commitment to the liberation of African, working, and oppressed people. Du Bois appealed to prominent Black leaders to petition the United States President and Attorney General to immediately pardon his "fine and distinguished" comrade.

Like Du Bois, Hunton, was one of the great Pan-Africanists of the twentieth century. Numerous organizations, publications, movements, and struggles benefitted from his deep knowledge of the African continent, steadfast commitment to ending colonialism and imperialism, protracted struggle to eradicate Jim Crow and apartheid, excoriation of fascism in its many forms, challenge to colonialism and corporate domination, and vision of a socialist world devoid of the violence and inhumanity wrought by capitalist exploitation. Hunton was courageous, humble, hardworking, and ethical, and never wavered from his commitment to the working and oppressed people of the world—not least those of African descent. His scholarship and praxis thus stand the test of time and remain especially relevant to a world still suffering from many of the forms of exploitation and oppression that he challenged up until his dying day.

Hunton's third wife, Dorothy, is largely responsible for the preservation of his legacy. *Alphaeus Hunton: The Unsung Valiant,* was the first—and remains the only—full-length treatment of his life and immense contributions to the freedom and liberation struggles aimed at remaking a world plagued by Euro-American ruling class domination. While his papers, which Dorothy Hunton gifted to the Schomburg Center for Research in Black Culture in 1985, are the premier source for information about his multifaceted work, her labor of love—the "modest tribute to a unique and noble man"—nonetheless remains an important reference for scholars interested in an intimate and detailed depiction of his life. Indeed, *Unsung Valiant* provided the basis for later profiles of Alphaeus Hunton, including "W. Alphaeus Hunton (1903-70)" in *Pan-African History: Political Figures from Africa and the*

Diaspora since 1787 edited by Hakim Adi and Marika Sherwood (2003) and Tony Pecinovsky's "W. Alphaeus Hunton: The National Negro Congress, the Council on African Affairs and Black Liberation" in *Let Them Tremble: Biographical Interventions Marking 100 Years of the Communist Party USA* (2019). It is also cited throughout important texts examining the intersections of anti-imperialism, anticolonialism, and Black liberation, including *Race Against Empire: Black Americans and Anticolonialism, 1937-1957* (1997), *Sojourning for Freedom: Black Women, American Communism, and the Making of Black Left Feminism* (2011), and *The Path to a Greater, Freer, Truer World: Southern Civil Rights and Anticolonialism, 1937-1955* (2014). With this re-printing of *Alphaeus Hunton: The Unsung Valiant,* it is my hope that many more scholars, organizers, and activists will not only become familiar with a man who, according to Du Bois, had an unmatched knowledge of the African continent, but will also commit themselves to the types of study and struggle that vivified Alphaeus Hunton's storied life.

Like his comrades Paul Robeson, Esther V. Cooper Jackson, and Doxey A. Wilkerson, Alphaeus Hunton belongs to what I call the "Tradition of Radical Blackness." The Tradition of Radical Blackness describes black communist, socialist, and leftist analyses of the structural and material conditions of local, national, and global blackness, and efforts to imagine and bring into being liberating possibilities for all oppressed people. It centers critical political economy analysis, attends to intraracial class conflict and antagonism, theorizes the international character of Blackness as a special condition of surplus value extraction, and strives for the eventual overthrow of capitalism. The Tradition of Radical Blackness, informed by and engaged with real world struggles, encompasses African descendants' multivalent and persistent anti-systemic and counterhegemonic challenges to political economies and legitimating discourses that sustain racialized and gendered exploitation, exclusion, dispossession, and class-based domination. It is often routed through or enunciated from within the US given the latter's importance to the development of the capitalist world-economy since the seventeenth century, rise to global hegemony starting in World War I and consolidated after World War II, histories of anti-black terror rooted in capitalist imperialism, and endemic antiradical liberal statist pedagogy.

Hunton's activism, movement building, organizing, and militant journalism fit squarely in the Tradition of Radical Blackness. He helped to organize the American Federation of Teachers local 440 at Howard University to ensure that workers there had a legitimate voice on campus. He was at the founding of the National Negro Congress (NNC), a militant Black labor organization, in 1936, and soon became a member of the National Executive Board and leader of the Washington, D.C. chapter. He launched sustained campaigns against police brutality in Washington DC to protect the bodily integrity and civil rights of Black and oppressed people. When the NNC and the International Labor Defense (ILD) merged into the Civil Rights Congress (CRC) in 1946, he became a trustee of the CRC bail fund, which was used to defend numerous targets of antiblack and anticommunist state repression. In 1943, Hunton followed in the footsteps of his close comrade Doxey Wilkerson and resigned from Howard University so that he could dedicate more time to the liberation of Africa, workers, and other poor, oppressed, and racialized people. He then became the educational director, and later the executive secretary, of the Council on African

Affairs (CAA). He edited the CAA's newspaper, *Spotlight on Africa* (previously called *New Africa)*, was a co-founder of the journal *Freedomways*, and contributed to several leftwing publications including *People's Voice, Freedom, Daily Worker, Political Affairs,* and *Masses and Mainstream.* He also became the head of the George Washington Carver School, the Harlem's branch of the Jefferson School of Social Sciences, an adult political education institution. Moreover, Hunton joined the Communist Party USA in the 1930s, not least because of their unabashed commitment to economic, social, and racial equality. He ended his life in Zambia after teaching in Guinea and, at the invitation of Du Bois, doing extensive work on the *Encyclopedia Africana* in Ghana. Hunton should therefore be considered among the likes of Du Bois, Robeson, William Patterson, and Angela Davis as a true champion of African, oppressed, working, and radical people.

Hunton's prolific writings offered lasting critiques of several structures of exploitation and oppression—not least capitalism, imperialism, colonialism, and war—to the Tradition of Radical Blackness. His vehement repudiations of capitalism illuminated how the expansion of the capitalist world-economy, constituted by surplus value extraction, labor exploitation, land and resource expropriation, and the perpetual accumulation of profit, especially relied upon the super exploitation of nations and peoples subjected to imperialism, colonialism, and antiblack racism. Likewise, like Vladimir I. Lenin, Hunton's writings conveyed that imperialism was the highest stage of capitalism in which the entire world was conscripted into the project of capitalist accumulation through processes of expropriation, dispossession, and plunder. For Hunton, imperialism was accompanied by the immiseration of the laboring classes of the world generally, and African populations particularly; increased militarism within national borders and between states; and the diminished ability of individual nations to pursue their own programs of political and economic development. Imperialism created relations of economic dependence between colonizing and colonized countries insofar as surplus value was transferred from the colonies to the metropole; the productive forces in the colonies were retarded; and colonies became an extension of foreign capitalist imperatives. Thus, imperialist powers were also colonial exploiters that, in parasitic fashion, sucked resources and labor from colonized nations for their own nourishment. This exploitation and oppression meant that colonized countries sacrificed the interests of their populations and their independent development to act as economic appendages to imperial capitalism. Moreover, Hunton demonstrated that imperialism fundamentally disrupted endogenous social relations by creating "comprador," landlord and parasitic bourgeois classes that were appendages of the international bourgeoisie. In effect, imperialism arrested historical development in Africa and throughout the Third World, the response to which was coordinated national revolutionary struggles for independence and self-determination. Throughout his writings, Hunton promoted peace and mutual cooperation because he understood that war and militarism were endemic in the above processes. Insofar as the accumulation of wealth in imperial countries required cheap labor from and expropriation of materials produced in poor countries, militarism legitimated the contravention of sovereignty and the mobilization of extraordinary violence in the service of plunder. The ruling elite and "labor aristocracy" in imperialist countries—especially the United States—supported perpetual war to defend their way of life and standard of living against populations on the darker side of the color-line and those who advocate the socialist redistribution of the world's wealth and resources. He showed that warmongering facilitated the drive for endless profit through the continual construction of enemies and threats that ostensibly menaced democracy, prosperity, freedom, and security. Often, these enemies were racialized and oppressed populations.

Pamphlets including *Stop South Africa's Crimes* (1946), *Seeing is Believing: The Truth about South Africa* (1947), and *Resistance Against Fascist Enslavement in South Africa* (1953), to which he contributed the postscript, excoriated every aspect of apartheid in South Africa, from the oppressive pass laws to the repression of unions and worker organizing to the abysmal working conditions and wages. He also identified the role of the United States, Europe, and international corporations in abetting and propping up the dehumanizing system. His pamphlets on the Bandung Conference, *Bandung: Asian-African Conference* (April 1955) and *Review of the Asian-African Conference* (May 1955) highlighted the historic nature of this gathering, which was planned by the governments of India, Indonesia, Pakistan, Burma, and Ceylon, and met from April 18-22, 1955. He noted that the conference explicitly excluded all European and American participation and had as its overarching principles nation-building, geopolitical autonomy, and world peace. He supported the Conference's aims of self-determination and the right of Asian and African nations to choose their own political and economic system. Additionally, in his relatively unknown book, *Decision in Africa: Sources of Current Conflict* (1957), which expanded on his pamphlet *Africa Fights for Freedom* (1950), Hunton offered a searing indictment of Euro-American looting, exploitation, and plunder of the African continent from the late nineteenth-century onward. With a wealth of empirical data, he traced the development and evolution of capitalist imposition through peonage in farming, deplorable working conditions and paltry wages in shanty towns, exorbitant looting in mining schemes, the entrenchment of dollar imperialism through private enterprise, and African dispossession resulting from European land grabs. Hunton also illuminated the long-term effects of these colonial patterns of production on the form and content of ongoing anticolonial protest and struggle saturating the continent. Hunton's intellectual production, which informed and was informed by his organizing and activism, offered a template for analyzing and challenging the biggest threats to human flourishing: capitalism, colonialism, imperialism, war, fascism, and white supremacy.

Given Hunton's dedication to the liberation of the oppressed, the colonized, and the world's otherwise exploited masses, the U.S. government worked tirelessly to marginalize and disgrace him. The Federal Bureau of Investigation, the Subversive Activities Control Board, the Attorney General's List of Subversive Organizations, and the House Committee on Un-American Activities, among other government entities, were used to continually harass, scrutinize, and disrupt his life and that of his comrades; to undermine and shut down his organizations; and to ultimately make his work exceedingly difficult, if not impossible. For example, in 1941, the Special Committee on Un-American Activities, chaired by the conservative Democrat Martin Dies, labeled the NNC's campaign for Black jobs at Glen Martin Aircraft factory subversive and claimed that Black communists aimed to sabotage defense production. Because he was the campaign leader, Hunton was branded a communist in order to discredit and to bring charges against him. Years later, the CAA and the CRC ceased operations due to government pressure, and Hunton was thrown in jail in 1951 for refusing to turn over the names of CRC donors. Some of his closest comrades, including Benjamin J. Davis, Jr., Claudia Jones, and Ferdinand Smith, were also indicted, incarcerated, and/or deported because of their political orientation and fearless activism.

It is my hope that the republication of *Alphaeus Hunton: The Unsung Valiant* will provide a new generation of scholar-activists with an intellectual, analytical, and political tool to help us understand the contemporary world situation. In the United States, on January 6, 20201, a mob of rightwing rioters stormed the Capitol building in Washington, DC to disrupt the official installation of the democrati-cally elected Joseph R. Biden administration. On November 6, 2020, India wit-nessed the largest general strike of farmers and workers in history to increase employment, wages, and food rations and to curb the tide of privatization and austerity. In Nigeria, #EndSARS protests erupted in late 2020 to dismantle the neocolonial Special Anti-Robbery Squad that had long wreaked havoc on ordi-nary citizens. In South Africa, xenophobia against displaced workers attempting to make a living is on the rise. In Haiti, protests against austerity, corruption, and unchecked government violence persist. All of this is happening in the context of the worldwide rise of rightwing populism; a global COVID-19 pandemic that is disproportionately ravaging racialized and oppressed populations; ongoing US sanctions against Venezuela, Cuba, Iran, Zimbabwe, and other nations that severely hamper their ability to serve their populations; an impending cold war between China and the United States; and an ever-increasing chasm between the world's richest corporations and individuals and the ordinary masses.

Many of these problems stem from the very issues Hunton challenged throughout his life: capitalist exploitation, imperial domination, coloniality, white supremacy, and perpetual war. As such, there is much to learn from his organization building, internationalist outlook, Pan-African commitment, and unrelenting efforts to realize a peaceful, socialist world. In the final analysis, Dorothy Hunton's chronicle of her late husband's life is also a template for the ongoing struggle for freedom and liberation.

Dr. Charisse Burden-Stelly

PREFACE

Since late afternoon, I had boldly resisted the cold and icy wind several times, and stood on deck, watching the billowy crest of the waves soar high in the air as the Farrell Line freighter dipped down, then up, splashing misty spray into my face and sending a chill through my body. The scene was fascinating yet terrifying. One could endure it only a short time. Alphaeus ventured out once, but quickly retreated to the warm comfort of the library to continue his work. January can be a bitter month on the high seas.

Our month-long voyage from Ghana was near its end as the ship glided by the stately Statue of Liberty. We had been deported, after the military coup overthrew the Ghanaian government. Nearly five years of hard struggle to get the **Encyclopedia Africana** off the ground were suddenly disrupted. The scholastic walls of Howard University, Washington, D.C., where Alphaeus taught for seventeen years, had been too constricting for his universal spirit. He chose to devote his life to the cause of African freedom, and for twenty-five years, he pursued that course.

The freedom of Africans was not, however, his sole concern. He was disturbed wherever injustices occurred; wherever man was denied his rights, and he went to prison in defense of his principles. Scholarship was no "Ivory Tower" for him. He believed in action on a wide variety of social, political and economic issues, and used his pen as well as his person in those objectives. Always calm and unruffled under the most trying conditions, Alphaeus never faltered, even in the face of death; a tireless worker, sympathetic and just, who gave little thought to his meager, personal needs. He was one of the unsung heroes of our time. Work was his life, and life was his work, and neither would be separated from the other.

About fifteen years have passed since I sat alone beside the bed of my beloved, numb with grief, holding his cold, emaciated hand in mine. Only the sound of his heavy breathing and the constant twittering of the busy little sparrows near the open window of our sunny home in Lusaka, Zambia, broke the almost unbearable silence. Suddenly, a strange guttural sound, a quick gasp, the last heave of his heavy heart, and he calmly and peacefully slipped into the great unknown.

The responsibility, with a persistent, gnawing urgency to record his eventful and disciplined life, I assume with a deep and abiding love and a desire to pay my modest tribute to a unique and noble man whose life it was my privilege to share for many years. It is my hope that his dedication will be an inspiration to others to heed the call to service. May it encourage them to feel deeply the needs of others; to participate in the never ending struggle for unity; that together they may build the new age world, filled with truth and beauty, for all to enjoy.

This book is in no way an attempt to deal in depth with the political and social persuasions that motivated Alphaeus's scientific approach to the problems of society. It is essentially my own evaluation of his life and work from the point of view of a wife and helpmate, and one who learned much about him while also learning much about the world in which we both lived.

It is to the scholarly historian and biographer of the future, to one knowledgeable in the intricate patterns of the social systems of our time, that I look for a more comprehensive account of Alphaeus's life, in which all aspects of his varied activities will be seen in their proper relation. A presentation of such depth I am unable to give.

Throughout the nearly four years of fascination and frustration that mingled with my efforts to put Alphaeus's life together, many encouraging friends made available information, suggested sources, criticized portions of the manuscript, and in other ways gave me a lift.

A special thanks goes to Dr. Dorothy Porter, curator of the Moorland-Spingarn collection at Howard University who gave hospitality and assistance when I journeyed to Washington to interview Alphaeus's colleagues, and to George B. Murphy Jr., a warm friend of long standing, a Contributing Editor of Freedomways, and on the staff of the Afro-American newspapers who never failed to answer a call for help.

To Dr. John Lovell, Jr., Dr. Sterling Brown, Dr. Rayford Logan, my niece Roberta Williams, Dr. James W. Butcher and Dr. Philip Butcher, Dr. Herbert Aptheker, William L. Patterson and Dr. Doxey Wilkerson, thank you.

CHRONOLOGY

1863   William Alphaeus Hunton, Sr., born in Chatham, Ontario.

1903   William Alphaeus Hunton, Jr., born September 18, in Atlanta, Georgia.

1906   Vicious race riot in Atlanta. Family moved to Brooklyn, New York.

1926   Appointed assistant professor of English at Howard University, Washington, D.C.

1936   Helped to organize the Washington Council of the National Negro Congress.

1943   Married at Alexandria, Virginia.

1951   Sentenced to prison for contempt of court.

1955   Council on African Affairs closes.

1957   Wrote *Decision in Africa.*

1959   Attended the All African People's Conference in Ghana.

1960   Moved to Guinea, West Africa.

1962   Went to Ghana, to work on the *Encyclopedia Africana.*

1963   Set up Regional Committees in North and East Africa.

1966   Deported from Ghana.

1967   Returned to Africa - Zambia.

1970   Died January 13, in Zambia.

1. THE BEGINNING

At the dawn of the Nineteenth Century the western section of the Province of Ontario, Canada, was virgin forest, teeming with roving Indians. That natural state ended aburptly when the British seized vast areas of that rich agricultural territory around 1759, and the first white settler, William Chrysler, built his small log hut. The enormous variety of fine-grained timber, the farming opportunities, attracted many rugged pioneers to the new region, and the small settlement called Chatham grew rapidly.

In the United States, the baneful system of slavery had spread its slimy tentacles over the entire southern region. Its decadent parasitic society, living lavishly off the sweat and imposed degradation of slave labor, had by its very character, united the humanitarian elements of the nation that formed the inconspicuous power behind the well organized "Underground Railroad." Escape to the North from the claws of humiliating servitude, through devious by-paths and detours, was perilous and meant certain return to bondage. By the middle of the Nineteenth Century, at least seventy thousand slaves had crossed the border into Canada. One of those was Stanton Hunton.

Stanton Hunton was the slave of a kindhearted woman of the Virginia aristocracy. Miss Nettie was not only his owner, but a relative, since he was fathered by a member of her family. That situation was not unusual. Slave owners ravished their female slaves at will. More often than not, those offspring lived in the "big house," and some came to consider themselves better than the field slaves. As they were mulattoes, and were a mite higher in the master's estimation, the sinister influence of color consciousness (which exists to some extent today) crept into the minds of many light-colored slaves. Miss Nettie was, however, fond of Stanton, and though it was illegal to teach slave to read and write, she secretly assisted his education from early childhood, so that he grew up an intelligent youth.

Realizing the difficulty of holding him after he had made three unsuccessful attempts to flee, she reluctantly agreed to let him buy his freedom in 1840. Immediately, he left Virginia, and with help, Stanton cautiously made his way to Chatham, where he built his humble home among other settlers, many of whom, like himself, were freed slaves, or fugitives.

Not satisfied with obtaining his own freedom, he returned to the United States and negotiated for the freedom of his brother Ben, who was a slave in Natchez, Mississippi. His efforts were successful, but Ben was unable to survive the severe climate in Ontario, and soon succumbed. Desolate and overcome with grief, Stanton made another trip to the U.S., this time to Cincinnati, Ohio, where he married Mary Ann Conyer, a beautiful Cincinnati girl, and with her returned to Chatham, the tiny village he was eagerly helping to build.

Chatham is remembered as the little town, on the Thames river, in which the humanitarian, John Brown, with his small band of courageous comrades, mapped strategy for the daring blow against slavery in Harper's Ferry, Virginia; one of the most electrifying episodes in American history. It shocked the nation and the world. This served as a deafening call to Blacks and their white abolitionist friends who viewed it as a startling inspiration and the oncoming scourge of the Civil War. Though John Brown had visited other towns in the area, he chose to stay in Chatham in 1858, perhaps because it was centrally located; was known for its enterprising and industrious citizenry; and was very close to the equally energetic settlement of Buxton, which was founded in 1848, by the Rev. William King, with fifteen former slaves as a nucleus.

Few people knew the real purpose of John Brown in Chatham and those who did were pledged to secrecy until he made a trip to the United States and returned with those fearless leaders who were to follow him, even unto death. Stanton Hunton, however, was one who knew. A deeply religious man, he was committed to the urgent task of giving himself unstintingly to the activities of the Abolitionist Movement. He made his home a station on the treacherous road to freedom, and was a close friend of John Brown. The small group often met at his home, where discussions were held and plans drawn up for that fatal attack on Harper's Ferry. Hunton was one of the quiet, dedicated members of the group, called to a conference by John Brown that May 8th, 1858, in Fire Engine House Number 3. One member of the Conference wrote:

> There was scant ceremony at these proceedings by these earnest men. They were of two colors, but one mind, and all were equal in degree and station here. No civic address to this Canadian town; no firing of guns was heard; no beat of drums. The place was rude and unadorned, yet the object of this little parliament was the freedom of four million slaves. [1]

"A table at which John Brown sat and wrote has been preserved in the family," Addie Hunton wrote in the biography of her husband, "but the Hunton's homestead at King and Willington St., known still as 'Hunton's Corner,' is the present site of the Canadian Pacific Railroad. The later Hunton home still stands, however, plain, but sturdy and dignified, like the early owner." [2]

Three years after the first shots were fired that marked the beginning of America's bloody Civil War, William Alphaeus Hunton, one of a large family, was born October 31, 1863, in Chatham. His mother died when he was a small boy, and his six brothers and two older sisters were supervised by a wise father and sister, and for a while, a stern but devoted maternal grandmother.

Hunton's father, who believed that boys should be systematically industrious, allocated work to each child. One filled lamps, another cut wood for heating and cooking, while others scrubbed floors, swept the yard, and of course, cleared away the snow in winter. If chores ran short, he thought nothing of having the boys change a pile of bricks he kept for his work as a brick-mason, from one section of the yard to another just to keep them busy. In addition to their school work and other chores, there was a store and a hall, left largely to the sons to manage. Still, there was time for fun with school pals, who invariably called him "Billie," a name he loved his intimates to use, but one his wife, years later, could never voice. Such discipline, implanted by his early training, provided a valuable asset to William Hunton in his extremely active career.

There was a deep Puritan strain in the stern gospel of duty and Christian observances upheld by the Hunton household. Tradition and custom were not to be tampered with, and each child was compelled to hew the line. Yet, it was William, who practiced so faithfully the Christian virtues of his father, that his brothers dubbed him "The Parson." He taught the men's Bible class in Sunday School and his father was a member.

William Hunton's education was the best his period offered; he finished high school, graduated from Wilberforce Institute in Ontario, and later taught in the public schools of Dresden, Canada, near his home town. Teaching was not his preferred vocation, however, but an opportunity for work. He ardently desired to study for the ministry, and he hoped a way would open to pursue that objective. With that in mind, he resigned after a brief term, and was appointed a clerk in the Department of Indian Affairs in Ottawa. Though the teaching experience in Dresden had been short, he realized in later years, that in several ways it had been a valuable part of his education. Three years later, January 1888, he left for Norfolk, Virginia, the cradle of American slavery. In that poor, undeveloped area of the country, continually obsessed by race, he began his duties as the first paid Black Secretary of the Young Men's Christian Association.

Taking that position posed a momentous decision for Hunton, and his first impulse was to reject the offer. He knew, with acute dismay, the skeptical attitude of his entire family as to the wisdom of his judgment in entering upon that untried field, which offered neither security nor position. There would certainly be little time for intellectual pursuits, he thought, and perhaps the mission would be fraught with misunderstanding and more or less ostracism. On the other hand, he was torn between the desire for the unknown, with his pioneering spirit urging him on, and the need to keep the love and companionship of those in Ottawa.

Twenty-five was rather young for one to lead such a bold project. However, Hunton brought with him knowledge and seriousness that commanded respect, and even deference. Above all he was deeply consecrated to a religion that proved vital to his life and needed a wider scope of activity in which to express its tenets in a more definite and practical manner than his former position provided.

One wonders if the path of the new branch would have been easier had it been possible to initiate the Y.M.C.A. work during the Reconstruction period (1865-1877) following the Civil War. Great changes were in the making then; the war had settled one problem and created others. The constitutions of the reconstructed states were liberalized, for a short period after the southern barons were crushed. Yet, the Association put forth no attempt on behalf of Black men.

New systems of education were established, and encouraging strides were made in social legislation. At the same time, Blacks, together with white colleagues, shared political power in the Reconstruction Government. It was the first and only encounter with democracy the Government has ever experienced.

Hunton arrived on the scene ten years later when the tenor of life had already reversed itself, and ran in new, but muddy and treacherous channels. The defeat of Reconstruction, caused by the compromise between northern capitalist and southern feudal aristocracy had already left a bitter legacy for the lowly southerner in the form of economic slavery. Sharecropping, wretchedness, low wages, deplorable housing with a scarcity of the simplest facilities, and schools that defied description, had become a way of life.

With no previous contact with race prejudice, Hunton's gentle sensibilities underwent quite a shock on his first impact with segregation and its attending evils in the South. Ottawa's free environment and open friendliness had not prepared him for that sharp contrast, which cut him deeply. But he slowly adjusted and soon took the discrimination in stride; doing what had to be done and making no issue of the hardships and loneliness of that period. "It was all in a day's work," he commented.

The few small rooms over a store shortly became a center of interest for young Black men of the city. There were debating and literary societies, educational classes and athletic work (with little or no apparatus). Gradually they acquired a library as hundreds of donated books filled the empty shelves in response to a long list of books needed that was sent to friends and well wishers. In 1890, Hunton received a call to become the Secretary of the Colored Men's Department of the International Committee, and he quickly accepted it. The two years in Norfolk had been filled with failures and successes, frustrated desires for larger and better results; but also a conscious knowledge that a remarkable change for the better was taking place in the lives of the men he served.

The work with the International Committee required considerable traveling, which provided an opportunity to see the South, meet Association men, and observe their accomplishments which centered largely in schools. It also had the effect of deepening Hunton's previous conviction of the value of the movement for the men of his race, while still retaining his inclination for the ministry.

The trips across the country, and especially the South where he came face to face with the stark injustices to which Blacks were constantly subjected, distressed him immensely. Though Hunton had been able to break through many strong fortifications of race prejudice, he labored under no illusions relative to the rough, uncertain path ahead, nor the varied, painful causes retarding the work.

While in Norfolk he met Addie Waite, a lively, strong-willed young woman, who was born in Norfolk, though she seldom remained at home during his early activities. Addie was educated in the public schools of Boston, Massachusetts; the College of the City of New York and Kaiser Wilhelm University, Strassburg, Germany. A sociologist, she taught at A. and M. College of Alabama, and for a while in Norfolk.

It was in the summer of 1890 that her father, who had become one of Hunton's staunch supporters, welcomed his offer to accompany her as far as Cincinnati and put her on the train to Xenia, where she would visit her sister at Wilberforce University, while he would continue his lonely journey to Chatham. Young girls rarely traveled unaccompanied at that time. Chaperons were the order of the day. And was this one alluring! Hunton was a vigorous-looking man; piercing dark brown eyes under bushy brows, a rather prominent nose, black hair, and a thick mustache hanging over the corners of his mouth. Ordinarily, the trip would have seemed long and tiresome, traveling alone, on the slow, uncomfortable, cinder-filled train. With pleasant company and stimulating conversation, the hours passed swiftly, and unnoticed, for the friendship of a lifetime was budding.

Railroads, like street cars in Virginia, had not yet been hit by the infamous "Jim Crow" laws. Nevertheless, they soon became an integral part of the Southern states structure. The "Colored coach," always placed directly behind the puffing engine, frequently was part baggage car.

Xenia came into view far too soon for the engaging couple. Although their heads were light and their stomachs empty, what did it matter? They had found each other, without ever having to make the faintest search. Three years after that exhilarating trip, Addie and William were married.

During those three years they wrote to each other almost daily, and Addie quickly realized how often they would be separated after marriage. If she were to be content, despite their intimacy of spirit, it would be essential to find some satisfying compensation for his long, and frequent trips from home. The only way out, she decided, was to make his life hers. That she did to a surprising degree, and found new avenues of rewarding service in the process.

With the acceleration of work Hunton's responsibilities multiplied tenfold by 1898, the arduous task of supervising the various activities alone became increasingly difficult. Immediate help was needed if the larger opportunities he envisioned in the years ahead were to be accomplished. To that end Jesse E. Moorland became the second Black Secretary of the International Committee of the Y.M.C.A. to labor among Black men.

Hunton devoted much of his time to the student field, which had always filled him with enthusiasm, now that Moorland's special assignment dealt with city Associations. He had a deep affection for students. The movement was already developing with greater speed than the power to control it, and he saw in the students the key to the problem of leadership. His warm friendly approach often disarmed them, while he negotiated some delicate situation. They occasionally felt the sting of his severe verbal thrashing, though a little healing oil was poured on the wounds he had purposely made.

Hunton, basically a serious, hard working man, knew how to relax and had a keen sense of humor, which was never obvious to strangers. Only intimates knew and delighted in his jokes and pranks. His wife related that he took her to see a Wild West Show in which Buffalo Bill was the main attraction. "Great was my surprise and gone was my feeling of awe when Mr. Hunton yelled, whistled, clapped his knees, and waved his hat with the abandon of all other fans there. He would recover just long enough to apologized for his over-exuberance and then go off again."[3]

From the beginning of Moorland's association with Hunton, a warm, friendly relationship developed, and many letters were exchanged. At times his letters to Moorland expressed his "longing for some of his buoyant and hopeful spirit." Despite ever-present problems, he found great pleasure in teasing his "old friend," as seen by the letter he wrote from Talladega College, Alabama, on February 8, 1896.

My dear brother,

I have desired to write you ever since I left you in my "palace car" of equal accommodations etc. I asked the conductor if that was the car provided for colored people. He said, yes, I suppose so, then said it should be used by them only. Whereupon he marched that gang of convicts into the smoking car, much to my relief.

Have no time to write a letter, but I want to have the pleasure of presenting you with that hat. Poor folks should not be extravagant, so I hope you will be able to satisfy yourself with the enclosed twenty-five cents.

I hope someday to be able to show my full appreciation of your hospitality by furnishing you with cornbread and molasses under my own vine and fig tree. You know that Virginians have made themselves famous for making old-time ashcakes. Come along and don't fail to bring Mrs. Moorland with you. Tell Miss Kate to get married and bring her husband to visit us...[4]

One of the most significant achievements of Hunton's entire career was in the realm of race relations. What men thought of him caused no deep concern, but how profoundly he could impress them with his convictions on the brotherhood of man. There were times, in the latter years of his struggles, when he found it absolutely necessary to defend the principles he had affirmed earlier. Pettiness and narrowness upset him; confrontations always left him depressed. But he was prepared to undergo anything and everything for the best interest of the work. And not once did he have the desire to give up the task, rather he felt compelled to push forward.

As the only Black member of those early conferences of the International Secretaries, he longed for a larger representation from his own Department, and its absence caused him much anxiety. His efforts to lift human relations above restrictions of race and creed were constant and earnest; and because there were no selfish or arrogant qualities in his leadership, he was strikingly successful.

In 1899, the Huntons decided to settle in Atlanta, Georgia, the bustling university city in the heart of the racist, conservative South. This move offered a better opportunity to supervise student activities. It was in this city that their son Alphaeus was born, on September 18, 1903, the fourth child, and the second son to be named after his father. The first died in infancy, three years after the death of a daughter, Bernice, the first born of Addie and William Hunton.

The fall of 1906, a period many would like to forget, added another besmirched page to the existing tarnished history of the bigoted South. In Atlanta, the rumblings of previous upheavals suddenly erupted into one of the most vicious and appalling race riots that ever engulfed a people.

To soothe their fears that social equality might develop, whites passed segregation laws, primarily as a defense mechanism. The code of social conduct which prohibited Blacks from living in specific areas, and denied their use of certain public places, was more significant than the segregation laws that acted as a restraining force to maintain separation of the races.

As Blacks poured into the southern cities, after the farm economy broke down, relations between the races became more strained, and segregation laws became more rigid. At the same time, job competition grew along with rising feelings that were aided and abetted by hordes of the Ku Klux Klan who did the dirty work of the southern ruling class.

The Huntons had lived in Atlanta for eight years; now frustrated and distressed, in the wake of the rioting mobs, they saw a dubious future in Atlanta. Hunton was preparing to leave for Tokyo to attend The World's Student Christian Federation Conference - a trip that had filled his mind with intense anticipation for nearly three years. Now, this cruel outburst of unconcealed hatred and racism had left him stunned.

How could he leave his wife and small children alone and unprotected in such hostile surroundings, while he journeyed halfway around the world? It would not be easy to abandon the modest, comfortable home they had lovingly built. The most devastating realization came with the knowledge that they, as Blacks, had absolutely no rights as citizens; and though their lives were in jeopardy from the malicious acts of the rioting masses, indoctrinated with racial animosity - who cared? This sober fact left them only one choice - close the house and remain up North until his return. This decision made, they moved to Brooklyn, New York. Little did they know that the break would be final.

During Hunton's twenty-five years of dedicated service, he participated in three notable assemblies of widespread importance which had a far-reaching effect upon the Associations under his immediate direction.

The first was the Golden Jubilee of the Y.M.C.A. held in London in the summer of 1894. Its founder, George Williams, was knighted by Queen Victoria, to honor his world-wide achievement in developing a new unified and active Christian force. It was Hunton's first trip abroad, and the occasion was filled with exciting events, exploring various cities in England, a short jaunt to Paris, Brussels and Antwerp, then back to London where he gave a brief speech at the All-American dinner. The delegates from all over the world, who witnessed the pomp and ceremony, numbered more than nineteen hundred. For a while, caste and class distinction seemed wiped out in the blending of rich and poor, high and low, diverse nations, tongues and tribes. The adventure thrilled Hunton, and he delighted to relate in detail all he saw and heard to any interested listener.

The second event took place in Tokyo. One of six delegates from the U.S., Hunton left New York February 22, 1907, to join others from the four corners of the world, to attend The World's Student Christian Federation Conference. During the entire trip until his return in June, he kept a diary, a lucid picture of his observations and remarkable scenes along the way.

His speech, for which he had been gathering data for more than two years, was far-reaching in its reference to religion, education and economics of the African world. It was delivered to a very attentive and appreciative audience, and many were brought to tears by his eloquent delivery. The convincing appeal of his address prompted the Association to publish it in New York in pamphlet form for distribution throughout the states.

Interspersed among the many sessions were receptions, garden parties, luncheons and teas amidst much luxury and strange, compelling beauty. The short missionary tours he took with one of the many small groups of Western delegates were of more significance. They afforded an opportunity to see sections of the country that could not be seen otherwise. The patience and endurance of the Japanese, who sat on their feet for hours, in rapt attention and perfect comfort during the meetings, which were held in every city visited, always amazed Hunton.

On March 20, he sailed for China; there he attended the China Centenary Missionary Conference in Shanghai. Hunton was much impressed by the conference, but the teeming, noisy crowds of hopelessly poor and illiterate masses, dirty, half-clad men striving desperately with each other for a job, for which they would receive a few pennies, drew heavily upon his sympathy.

This eastern voyage proved to be the most broadening and strengthening experience of his life. The strangeness of the land and its people enchanted him; the vastness and mysterious aura of China thrilled him; but he would remember forever the misery of millions of poverty-stricken peasants he beheld at every turn, for whose relief from wretchedness he saw little hope.

Far removed from the hubbub of a frustrating society, beautiful Lake Mohonk, snuggling close to Sky Top Mountain, in New York State, and twelve-hundred feet above sea-level, was a perfect site for a quiet retreat. This spot was chosen in 1913 for the gathering of more than three hundred delegates from forty countries to the tenth Conference of The World's Student Christian Federation. For Alphaeus's mother and father, it was one of the happiest weeks of their married life. Completely free from the cares of the outer world, they experienced a more perfect communion of spirit than at any previous time. Hunton, as leader of the Black delegation, was alert to its needs and participation, and his positive yet gentle guidance was much in evidence.

At the close of the conference, he made the last public address of his career, a masterful appeal for the all-inclusive brotherhood of man. In conclusion he said,

> Pray with us that there shall come to the heart of the world, not only an intellectual interpretation of the brotherhood of man but a spiritual acceptance of it, so that speedily there may dawn a glorious morning when man shall not judge his fellowman by color, race, tradition or any of the accidents of life but by righteousness and truth and unselfish service to humanity. [5]

His strenuous life was now taking its toll. Racked by ill health from frequent bouts of tuberculosis, and often depleted and exhausted from overwork, Hunton suddenly collapsed after a trying situation in connection with the Young People's Christian Congress in Atlanta. Because he had labored long and hard, far beyond the call of duty, his perseverance and dauntless courage had enabled him to blaze the trail of true fellowship far better than he knew. Near the close of his declining years, Hunton remarked to his wife, in discussing the varied aspects of his work, "I really had no choice. It was God's leading, and I had but to follow."

> ...For his own sake William Alphaeus Hunton would have been the consideration of the people in any line of work he might have attempted to do. The outstanding fact about him was his sweet temper and brotherly spirit...His personality and spirit permeated the student bodies of our colleges and the men in the cities. His influence was felt wherever he was heard, and his name was precious in the life of the brotherhood. He proved himself a patient, wise leader in establishing confidence in the leadership of the race and movement...No one can half measure the debt the work owes to the poise and character of William Alphaeus Hunton, who for so many years stood as the lone representative of the race in this field. [6]

A vital segment of Addie Hunton's thinking included the theme that women have an important, creative role to play in improving the human welfare in their community. It was natural that she would be a delegate to the first meeting of the National Association of Colored Women when it met at the 19th Street Baptist Church, Washington, D.C., in 1896. Addie served on the Ways and Means, and Auditing Committees, and in 1906, and 1908 was elected organizer.

For more than a decade, Addie did most of her husband's secretarial work, and accompanied him to conferences whenever possible, taking care of the endless details, counseling and encouraging him. Her closeness to him and his activities during those arduous years marked her as one with striking qualities, a forerunner among Black women by the National Board of the Young Women's Christian Association. They finally began to notice their darker sisters.

Since Addie's restlessness always kept her in the vanguard for women's rights, she gave three months special service to their new program for Colored Students Associations in 1907. From that experience, she became the first Black worker and pacesetter for the Y.W.C.A. to labor among women of color. Through her activities more and better opportunities became available to improve their distressing way of life. Within a year after her survey, the roll of the Association doubled in schools on government and private foundations in fifteen states.

At the conclusion of three months of intensive effort, Addie suggested in her report a number of proposals necessary to the growth of the organization, with special emphasis on the need to discover and train leaders and secretaries. That resulted in the placement of four Black girls in the training course for employed leadership in 1911, for the first time. Commenting on that achievement, she said, "the effect of the summer course upon the public will be helpful in that it demonstrates the interest of the National Board in promoting the Association's movement among Colored women." [7]

In spite of having been employed specifically for student activity, Addie rendered valuable service in the cities as well. With others, she helped to organize the first conference of Black employed and volunteer city workers in New York City, June 1912. In addition, she gave eight addresses before The National Federation of Colored Women's Clubs, lyceums and other groups.

Conditions under which women worked in the factories and mills in the North as well as the South, in the early nineteen hundreds, bordered on the level of slave labor. Long hours, unhealthy surroundings and starvation pay were the plight of all. The industrial survey of that deplorable situation in the South, Addie Hunton undertook in the spring of 1912. Three thousand women working in Winston-Salem, portrayed "a picture of deep shadows, a story too dark, too depressing, too long to be unfolded here," her first report stated. "I have hope that a few colored women will take the initial steps in an effort to change the fearful current of life into safer channels...Here a house originally intended for a center is in disuse for want of leadership." [8]

The results of that inspection compiled by Addie were published by the Association under the title, "Beginnings Among Colored Women." To the end of her life she continued to serve as an active member of the National Board.

The continuously widening horizons of the Y.M.C.A. assumed such extensive proportions, and required so much travel, that the work curtailed sharply the time Hunton could spend with his family. He loved them deeply, and yearned for the companionship of his wife and lively, carefree hours with the children especially Eunice, his vivacious daughter. As the most exuberant member of the family, she could always be relied on to keep her father lighthearted and gay. His infrequent homecomings were precious events, invariably creating a storm of excitement, affection and fun, which quickly relieved the strain of his soaring problems and anxieties. If it were vacation, and there was ample time for play, a jolly family picnic highlighted his stay. Alphaeus, the serene, contemplative one, with his growing inwardness and withdrawal even in his tender years, was seldom demonstrative, and never hilarious. Yet, he delighted in his father's occasional spurts of gaiety, and quiet, colorful humor. His greatest enjoyment from those memorable occasions was the paternal encouragement and help he received in his studies during the rare moments of intense enthusiasm they shared together.

From the outset, books and learning interested Alphaeus more than anything else. He would read all night if he were not found out, or deprived of light. And he was strong-minded. No one ever changed his mind for him, or tried any silly horseplay at school. A born scholar, his mother thought. Like his father, he practiced the rare art of communicating with himself, and never seemed to tire of being alone with his reflections. It was, therefore, no surprise to find him thoroughly enjoying the debating society at Boys High School in Brooklyn, New York, and not particularly impressed by the frequent overtures of the captain of the football team. In 1918, he helped organize and became the secretary of an organization of Black high school students, dedicated to "higher scholarship," Alpha Chi Sigma.

When Alphaeus was six, Addie took him and Eunice to Germany, where she studied at Kaiser Wilhelm University in Strassburg. Both children went to school and soon spoke German well. This early exposure to that gutteral language influenced him in later years to continue the study of German. Though he hardly ever spoke it, he made excellent use of his knowledge for reading and research.

The trio remained in Europe two years, spending several months in Switzerland. Unfortunately, Addie was unable to finish her course. The persistant, disturbing thought that her husband might be ill, would not leave her. She knew his enthusiasm was often unequal to his strength. Several years previous, malaria had racked his system for many months and so devastated him that he never completely overcame its effect. Exposure to the hazardous conditions of traveling in remote sectons of the South had further weakened his constitution, along with his own neglect of his health from overwork. Knowing that, she returned to Brooklyn, and realized immediately that her thoughts were not unfounded. In spite of two minor operations after her hasty arrival, Hunton never overcame a chronic, hacking cough, that continually plagued him, the result of tuberculosis of the throat.

Alphaeus's young years were spent in an atmosphere of freedom to grow and explore. Discovery was a way of life. Yet, the ordinary, mischievous diversions of the neighborhood boys seldom enticed him. To indulge in their frivolity and escapades did not come easily, for a serious view of life had already taken hold. Nevertheless, there were times when the allure of excitement was too great, and like any normal, healthy boy, he joined in vigorous sports. The choice of activity was his to make, and the choice, more often than not was connected with books.

In the Huntons' home, there was no end to the variety of books, in their well-chosen library, through which he could rummage to his heart's delight. There were books to stimulate the mind and excite the imagination; to travel in other regions and times with captivating companions while he sprawled in the living room chair with his long legs dangling on the floor and his eyes riveted to the page. At thirteen, his beanpole body had reached six feet and was destined to grow another four and a half inches before it stopped. Such height caused him to stoop, in a desire to appear shorter than he was. His mother kept reminding him to pull his shoulders back, and walk like his father, who, though not quite as tall, never stooped, but carried himself with regal stateliness.

Alphaeus knew that his father's love of beauty carried over into literature, and he often gave him a book for Christmas. Most of the books purchased and read by William Hunton, however, were on Africa, that so-called dark, and mysterious continent, that so few people had knowledge of, and few cared anything about. He was keenly interested in the plight of his African brothers, and rarely did he give a speech that he did not plead fervently for the extension of the Y.M.C.A. movement to that vast and ageless land. Frequently, he discussed with his wife the manifold problems facing the Africans, and no doubt Alphaeus was near asking questions, or just listening. Little did anyone realize that the seeds of those talks would take root, grow deep and strong, and years later, finally push him out of the relatively secure position at Howard University, to flower in the struggle for human dignity and freedom.

The splendor of that crisp, spring morning in 1918, brought none of the usual promise of adventure to Alphaeus, a lad of fourteen, and Eunice. Uncertainties and fears over-shadowed them as they stood on the crowded pier with relatives and friends, smiling through their tears, waving goodbye to their mother. A year and a half ago, their father had died, now their mother, one of three Black women, was sailing for France. They would serve on the war front of World War I, as canteen workers and secretaries in the Women's work for the War Council of the Y.W.C.A. Would she return, or be numbered among the casualties of battle?

The United States had declared war on Germany in 1917, and thousands of troops had been sent overseas. However, the War Department would accept no Black volunteers. None could serve in the Air Force, Coast Guard, or Marine Corps. The sole exception was the Navy, which admitted Blacks as messmen, only. With the acceleration of the war, they were drafted and compelled to bear arms in segregated units, mostly as dock hands and other service contingents.

Fifteen months of near continuous service carried Addie over practically all of France. She lived through agonizing fears, and often worked from early morning to midnight. Hers was an ever changing, uncertain camp life made more difficult and frustrating because of insufficient help and the deep rooted prejudices of white, southern officers, who took every opportunity to show their authority and arrogance.

After many months at the front, amid the desolation and confusion of combat, Addie went to southern France to minister to the sick and weary Black soldiers who came for rest and recreation, surrounded by the cool, towering, majestic Alps. From the trials and feelings of that wartime encounter, she co-authored with Kathryn M. Johnson, an interesting book, **Two Colored Women with the American Expeditionary Forces.** [9]

Throughout Addie Hunton's busy life, she was an integral part of numerous clubs, organizations and committees, and she raised her vibrant voice persistently at various national and international conferences. Her spirited nature propelled Addie into so many activities that family life was at times disrupted. During those periods, Eunice and Alphaeus made their home with the family's good friends, Mr. and Mrs. Harry Hairston in Brooklyn.

It was not until Hunton's serious illness, in the spring of 1914, when Addie took him to the little village of Saranac Lake, in the heart of the Adirondack region, that the family knew with certainty that tomorrow they would still be together. The lovely cottage, snuggled amidst so much beauty and serenity in the fastness of the mountains, was home for nearly a year and a half. Eunice remained at school in Brooklyn, and joined them for Christmas, but Alphaeus who was only eleven, stayed with his parents and continued school there.

Seldom had the opportunity occurred for Hunton and his son, both lovers of beauty, to become close and discover how much they could share and enjoy together. Now, there was time. Aside from the help his father gave with his studies, there were problems running through his young, serious mind to talk over when he put his books aside. Hunton was delighted, especially as he gained in strength, and Alphaeus accompanied him on short walks.

Winter was long and severe with the temperature falling, at times, thirty degrees below zero. Spring finally arrived, and with it renewed life. Since food prices were sky-high, the Huntons decided to have a vegetable garden. It would not only help their weakened finances, but afford some occupation and pleasure. Addie and Alphaeus took over the hard work, after a man with his horse and plow prepared the soil. Hunton, however, supervised everything from beginning to end. Not one plant missed his exacting eye. The harvest was far beyond their wildest dreams, despite the lack of encouragement from neighbors who thought the project was a rather bold enterprise. Not only did they raise enough vegetables for their own needs, "including corn, which the natives said could not be grown," but they also had some to spare for neighbors. In addition, the products won two blue ribbons and a $2.50 gold piece at the county fair. It was Alphaeus's first and last attempt at gardening.

Hunton's death, while the children were still in high school, posed a grave problem for their future education. Alphaeus worked many long, hot summer months as a redcap in Pennsylvania Station, The bags he carried were so heavy that they caused his right shoulder to droop, and made one arm two inches longer than the other. Nevertheless, like many Black youths in the same predicament, the hard work supplied the means to continue school.

William Alphaeus Hunton
Father

Addie Waite Hunton
Mother

Alphaeus Hunton

Eunice Hunton Carter
Sister

A friend, Addie, Alphaeus
Hot Springs, Arkansas

Alphaeus, Eunice
Brooklyn, N.Y.

A friend, Alphaeus, Addie
Great Barrington, Mass., 192

2. HOWARD UNIVERSITY

How deeply the compelling, spiritual power of William Alphaeus's quiet but dynamic personality permeated his son's inner sanctum and influenced his life is difficult to appraise. Though they pursued entirely different avenues of achievement, fundamentally their goals were the same: the uplifting of oppressed Blacks.

The elder Hunton derived his strength from daily devotional study of the Bible, meditation and prayer, and lived unwaveringly by faith. But this was not a blind faith without the sanctity of works, whose potency he endeavored to transmit to those he served. In contrast, the years of maturing in college, and the subsequent depression, convinced Alphaeus that the pressures and inequalities of the downtrodden could be relieved only through radical social change.

The Huntons were conservative, politically, and devoted Episcopalians. Alphaeus, like his father and grandfather, was brought up in the church, and served as an acolyte. Unlike them, he began to question the validity of religious teachings during his youthful resistance to tradition. Gradually, he weaned himself from the rigid Christian dogmas of his ancestors, as many of his day did, and the religious persuasions of his childhood seemingly vanished in the course of his intellectual development. His inclination for analytical deductions quickened his radical leanings and prevented his acceptance of an abstract philosophy. Alphaeus referred to himself as an agnostic, a "compromise between scientific materialism and idealistic faith." Yet, I doubt if he ever was completely free from the grip on his feelings that his early Christian training fostered.

On the other hand, if there was anything embedded in him from his conventional upbringing, it was a conviction that serving others is a moral obligation, together with a sense of indignation at the injustices caused by law and public opinion (which seems stronger than law in this country). "I may be slow and deliberate," he once said to me, "and go out of my way to avoid trouble that can be avoided, but nothing will stop me from getting what I go after, once I set my mind to it." That point Alphaeus amply exemplified throughout his life.

Years later, he had the occasion to work very closely with clergymen in numerous campaigns. For those who were leaders in social programs, and practiced in public the religious principles they professed in private, and were willing to have those principles tested in the crucible of public opinion, he had the deepest regard. While he could not accept religion himself, he respected the rights of others to enjoy it.

Alphaeus's interest lay in the social and economic structure of society, and its relationship to the underprivileged and forgotten man, rather than in the Christian ethics of institutionalized theology. He was concerned with a system of social organization in which there were equal opportunity, and freedom from economic exploitation of races, nations and classes. Experience had convinced him of the need to deal with the world as it was, especially the day-to-day problems that confronted the faithful believer, whose only happiness centered in the church, and its social activities. This is particularly true of the Black church, which traditionally has been more than merely a religious institution.

As the most promising means of making a living, Alphaeus sought a teaching position after receiving his M.A. from Harvard. In September 1926, he was appointed Assistant Professor at Howard University in Washington, D.C. Washington was then so tightly locked on the horns of race prejudice, that the Library of Congress was one of the few places Blacks could enter and feel relatively free from segregation. It ranked among the most undemocratic large cities in the country, and was riddled with Federal apathy on the color question, thus exerting an extremely negative influence on the nation by its racist example.

In that oppressive and warping environment, Alphaeus began to teach for $1800 a year. Having spent his college years there, he was no stranger to the subtle machinations of the citizens and the government. And he knew that whites could live a lifetime in Washington without becoming directly aware of the university. He also knew that the top-notch faculty and graduates in many fields were making their pressures felt, and would continue to work for changes in the national status quo until justice was achieved.

In the First Congregtional Church of Washington, D.C., on November 20, 1866, in a prayer meeting Howard University was born. Its intention was to train ministers of the gospel, but it gradually came to embrace all branches of knowledge for all races of men. The difficulty of finding a name for the institution posed quite a problem for the founders, but they finally accepted the name of the American philanthropist, the Commissioner of the Freedman's Bureau, General Oliver Otis Howard.

Without one cent in the treasury, the Normal Department opened on May 1, 1867, in a rented frame building with four students, daughters of two of the University founders.

> The first ten years were years of feverish growth, also years of marvelous faith. Suddenly, the panic of 1873 fell upon the country, and became nationwide. The Freedman's Bureau was abolished; individual and church support was withdrawn from the University-- as a result, income failed to meet expenses. Bankruptcy was ahead. In order to save the endowment, and valuable lands, a policy of economy and retrenchment was pursued...Emerging from that crisis, much reduced, but still intact, the university entered upon a slow, but healthy growth...

Now Howard is the largest Black university in the U.S., and teachers and students come not only from all parts of the states, but from foreign lands as well.

Three months before Alphaeus's appointment Howard took on a new image when Dr. Mordecai Wyatt Johnson, the first Black president, was elected. Dr. Johnson, a Baptist minister, held several degrees, and achieved an enviable record of constructive accomplishments. One, of prime importance, was obtaining legislation by which Howard became the responsibility of the U.S. Government, thus putting the University on a sound financial basis for the first time. That made it possible to revolutionize the physical plant by construction of several new and badly needed buildings. During his administration, teachers' salaries increased regularly along with the quality of the teaching staff, and conditions for teaching. Dr. Johnson unceasingly insisted upon high standards of scholarship, which paved the way for one of the most outstanding publication of its kind, **The Journal of Negro Education,** a quarterly review of problems incident to the education of Blacks.

I don't believe Alphaeus would have had the patience to be a good high school teacher. Dealing with very young, and often flighty youths would have frustrated his inherent and persistent passion for perfection, and put an unbearable strain on his tolerance. At times, he may have appeared cool, but inwardly, he would have been seething with annoyance or discomfort; he would have found it too embarrassing, however, to disclose his true feelings.

At Howard, Alphaeus was in charge of freshman English. The eager newcomers, particularly the girls, soon learned to their sorrow that the tall, handsome instructor with the cropped mustache, who bespoke gentle courtesy and refinement, would brook no nonsense in his class. A kind, but exacting disciplinarian, he was determined to make them improve their minds.

His movements displayed a quiet efficiency, as though he were conserving his energy for greater things. Never inattentive, or indifferent, he drew the maximum from his students because he himself was untiring. Yet, Alphaeus accorded praise cautiously, and sparingly. In class, or on paper, no slipshod phrases ever escaped his attention. Students had high respect for him for "he showed a keen interest in their problems as students in courses other than his own," and was ready to give assistance whenever he could, often talking to them by the hour. He kept his office door open so that no lack of student-faculty contact would arise.

With the serious students, Alphaeus established good working relations, but he could be severe and unbending with the naive pupil who believed he or she could float by without putting forth any worthwhile effort. A case in point was that of our friend Angie Taylor Dickerson.

Angie took public speaking in her freshman year. The course, an analytical study of various types of public addresses placed stress on speech briefs, and preparation and delivery of original speeches. Angie was an articulate speaker, and enjoyed the exhilaration of talking. During the semester, her work earned an A, but to her dismay, her final mark was B plus. Incensed, she rushed into Alphaeus's office to inquire why. After a few moments silence while he observed her perturbed expression, Alphaeus quietly said, "I'm sorry, Miss Taylor, but you made no improvement."

Rarely did Alphaeus take the opportunity to stroll across the room while making a point; he preferred to conduct his lectures in the century old, Victorian style, teaching from behind the desk. His lectures were far reaching in their content and import, still, to some, at times, they seemed a bit smothered by his rigid, scholarly discipline. And though his personality was not outgoing, it was not unfeeling. A disarming kind of shyness overshadowed him.

"At committee meetings of his department, or faculty," recalled Dr. John Lovell, Jr., a friend and colleague, "Alphaeus usually found himself at the end, as chairman. Careful and exacting in any duty to perform he could be relied upon to complete the job no matter what." His painstaking reports , which were a masterpiece of particulars, frequently amazed the members, as well as his ability to ferret out the cause at the root of a sticky and often irksome problem.

Yet, when he was not directly concerned with his work, Alphaeus's reserve and reticence gave to a few the impression of aloofness — characterizing him as anti-social. And he was to a degree. Friendly, albeit withdrawn, he displayed an element of exclusiveness. However, Dr. Sterling Brown, a personal friend with whom he shared an office, did not think "it was an attitude of disdain; it was only that he was uncomfortable with small talk.''

If he were not really interested, those around him aroused little attention, and his efforts of sociability seemed meager. It simply was not a part of his world. Few people were permitted to enter Alphaeus's intimate domain, but those who did found a warm, vital person, a creative thinker, and a scholar, who searched the depth of his humanity in an effort to find the sphere of activity that would serve his fellowman best.

He taught many English courses: Short story writing, Argumentation, Elements of expression, English Composition, Oral English for teachers (secondary schools and colleges), English literary criticism to the death of Dryden, The History of English Literature in outline from 1660 to the end of the 19th century, and Contemporary American Literature from the end of the 19th century to the present.

Most students found Victorian Prose of slight interest, with scant relevance to busy, twentieth century realism. The course was an intensive, critical study of the major prose writers of the Victorian era against the social, and historical background of the period. Students usually lacked enthusiasm for the grim materials required for study. One had to be deeply immersed in the times to discover the relation of each writer's thought to the social, political, scientific, and religious influence of the age, then appraise those factors that influenced their lives. Few were prepared to tackle that formidable task.

"There were only three of us in the course," recalled Dr. Philip Butcher, Dean of the Graduate School at Morgan State College in Baltimore, "and it met rather late in the afternoon." Dr. Butcher took the course because he felt he owed it to himself to sit in at least one of Alphaeus's classes, though his interest was limited at the time to recent American fiction. "I couldn't understand," he said, "how Dr. Hunton, whose interests were known to center on explicit contemporary problems, could ever have taken the time and trouble to become an authority on what seemed to me, a dull prose of very distant English gentlemen." Yet he greatly admired him for doing so.

Alphaeus frequently reminded the students that social and economic studies were essential for a better understanding of the literary background, no matter how boring. The Victorian epoch, however, had a subtle fascination for him. His years of study systematically enlarged his knowledge of the 19th century imperialist development of Britain, and proved indispensible in his future African research.

At the height of the dismal thirties, the aftermath of the 1929 bank failures, when American society was crushed by its anguish, students on many campuses, including Howard's fumed with agitation. As if the national crisis was not enough, the violent way society had tried to intimidate

Blacks, and keep them in a servile place by continued lynchings, burst out anew. The resurgence of lynchings had claimed twenty-four lives in 1933 alone. Students and professors, along with others, clamored for immediate passage of the Anti-Lynching Bill, and Alphaeus became a leader in the fight. The students' deep concern for the poor southern share-croppers brought some measure of relief from their misery. They always sat on the edge of starvation, in strict separation from the white world. Life had never been anything but a heritage of woe since the inception of that detestable system. Now, their condition had become extremely critical.

Political action took place on many fronts against the social and economic ills affecting Blacks, and those professors and students who participated were quickly labeled "Red." Though the New Dealers unraveled many of the economic knots strangling the weakened nation, their deep-seated prejudices and unwillingness to become involved in racial issues prevented any noteworthy achievements. During that period, Alphaeus helped to organize the Teachers' Union, Local 440 of the American Federation of Teachers (A.F. of L.), and soon became a thorn in the Administration's side. He always held an office — either president, vice-president or secretary.

The National Labor Relations Act (NLRA) usually called the Wagner Act, became a law in 1935, and was perhaps the most significant of all the New Deal legislation. It gave employees the right to organize and bargain collectively through representatives of their own choice, and helped to eliminate a major cause of industrial conflict. The law paved the way for a new wave of unionism. By 1937, union membership doubled. The trade-union scene had acquired a new look, however, due to the appearance of the Committee for Industrial Organization (CIO), that emphasized industrial unionism in place of the traditional craft-unionism policy of the American Federation of Labor (A.F. of L.).

"The labor-conscious Negro teacher in America has a special interest in the question of the affiliation of the American Federation of Teachers (AFT) with the CIO," Alphaeus wrote in an issue of the **American Teacher** in 1838. The problem was, **Shall We Affiliate?** a discussion forum on AFL-CIO affiliation for union members. That special interest arose from the fact that the CIO represented the first opportunity Black workers had had to become an integral part of the American labor movement — to fight for and share in the benefits of organized labor.

Under the obsolete craft union structure of the A.F. of L. there was no place for the great mass of unskilled Black workers. As a general rule the small minority of skilled and semi-skilled Black workers admitted to the Federation were isolated in weak, Jim Crow locals. As a consequence of that virtual exclusion of Blacks from the ranks of organized labor, both Blacks and white workers suffered. Alphaeus said:

It is not necessary to enter here into a discussion of the various forms of special exploitation of Black workers, or to demonstrate how this condition has operated against the white worker, whether through the vicious practice of employing Negroes as strike-breakers or through the more subtle manifestations of the divide-and-rule principle. This is an old story.

The CIO stands for the unionization of our millions of unorganized workers, black as well as white, unskilled as well as skilled. Its principle of industrial organization, the organization for all workers in a plant or industry upon an equal and democratic basis, means the realization of that complete unity of labor which in turn means a powerful labor movement... The record speaks for itself.

If these gains are possible among industrial workers they are also possible among white collar workers, professional workers, and teachers... Especially does it apply to the underpaid and tenureless Negro teachers in our schools and colleges. In education, as in other fields of labor there must be organization of all workers if there is to be effective union progress... The CIO can, and has already shown the way. It is time for the teachers to catch up with the vanguard of labor.

Alphaeus believed strongly in organization, and that "true education could not be divorced from action." For him, effective action was organized and concerted, and he allied himself with those forces — progressive labor movement in particular — "whose ultimate aims are the same as those of democratic education: Peace, security and progress for the peoples of the world."

Society seemed hopelessly bogged down in its misery, as hardships grew, and social unrest continued to spread. Frustrations and despair overwhelmed the students, but their force and energy also grew. New York University, where Alphaeus studied for his doctorate from 1934 to 1938, was considered left of center. The atmosphere on the campus was that of marked activity on the part of the left, which was dedicated primarily to the struggle against war and fascism that faced them, as well as the structural inconsistencies in government. Students and faculty members of many persuasions joined in.

Students across the country, who saw no future when they finished college — if they finished — shared a sense of urgency. The outlook was bleak indeed. Moreover, they were impatient with the older generation, and disillusioned by the discrepancy between the code of ethics transmitted at home, in school and church, and what they encountered daily in the outside world. Many became more and more militant as they continued to appeal for help and understanding. For the thirties had become, in truth, years of anguish and suffering for millions who had little hope in a brighter tomorrow.

Alphaeus's progressive outlook, strongly tinged with originality, took the form of advanced social and political opinions and beliefs, and caused him to view the world clearly, without many illusions. His awareness of the fundamental moral and social issues of his times was greatly sharpened by his close association with those who thought along more radical lines. He was immensely influenced by his dissertation instructor, Dr. Edwin Berry Burgum, a leading Marxist, and editorial board member of **Science and Society,** a scholarly Marxist journal. As a well-grounded, disciplined researcher bent on scientific analysis of the current economic problems, he was interested in the historical approach to the cause behind the dilemma in which the country found itself, and not in idealistic overtures. In some respects, however, perhaps Alphaeus was an idealist.

He understood the importance of the crucial role economics played in history, and began to delve seriously into Marxist-Leninist philosophy to enhance his understanding of the recurring economic crises that gripped not only America but a large section of the world. To be an idealist was easy as long as ideals were detached from action. Alphaeus preferred action.

Subsequently, he accepted Marxist principles as the way towards a greater socialization of humanity, a problem that occupied much of his thoughts. Social justice as well as social analysis gave him deep concern. And the fact that the richest nation in the world permitted millions of people to live below the official poverty level distressed him. Always searching for the truth, Alphaeus's methods were unceasingly those of a scholar, and he pursued his objective relentlessly, no matter how much he had to endure.

His doctoral dissertation, **Tennyson and the Victorian Political Milieu,** dealt with the poet's opinions of the current political scene. Tennyson was above all "deeply concerned with the preservation of law and order in the state, and with the broadening and strengthening of the empire." The thesis also examined the British empire theory, and its history during the second half of the 19th century, and its impact on the poet's thoughts and writings; the public reaction in England and America to this glorification of Britain's imperial role, and his influence in that area of thought upon contemporary British poets, including Rudyard Kipling. In the conclusion of his study, Alphaeus wrote:

If one attempted to read the history of Victorian politics solely through the opinions and writings of Tennyson, one would get a reasonably clear conception of the advancement of England as a world power, but a very vague and uncertain impression of anything else... Of the two chief movements in Victorian politics, that of democracy, and that of nationalism, only the latter engaged his full sympathy and interest...

Tennyson feared political innovations and popular government; he was for the most part insensitive to the struggles for national liberty abroad; he shrank from the task of considering fundamentals and proposed outworn remedies for present ills; he was progressive only in his championing of the cause of the empire. In all these respects he spoke for the politically dominant class in Victorian England.

Camp, 1944

3. TRANSITION

It was a warm, still, sultry evening in August 1939. Not a single green leaf stirred on the beautiful trees that grew majestically along Seventh Avenue in Harlem. The day had been exceedingly hot and murky. Dark, menacing clouds hovered low over the city most of the day, and promised at any moment to break asunder and bring cooling relief. Yet as the day moved dismally on, they slowly drifted by and finally faded away without offering a single drop of the much needed rain. The almost unbearable humidity felt more stifling and enervating than before.

Crowds of people filled the streets. Young and old strolled leisurely along the broad sidewalk. Some gathered in small groups chatting animatedly about the recent fire that took the lives of five young people. Children who should have been in bed hours ago were running and playing as if it were high noon, with no thought of tomorrow. Yet who wanted to go to bed in such heat? The thought of lying awake for hours, struggling to fall asleep in a stuffy apartment, was not a comforting one.

"Hello there!" A voice rang out amid the clatter of many voices as I hurried on my way home.

I turned in the direction of the greeting, thinking that the voice seemed vaguely familiar. There stood Alphaeus on the busy corner, looking tired and somewhat forlorn but with a wistful, soft look on his handsome face.

Many years had passed since he had visited our home one summer, paying court to my elder sister Edythe Scott. But vacation soon came to a close, and back to Howard he went, ending that short-lived, gay summer interlude. Time, and the inevitable searchings of youth to find oneself had pushed the memory of him into the deep recesses of my mind. Now, there he stood, tall and stately, looking down at me, with a mischievous twinkle in his dark brown eyes, sunk deep under their brows, and the ever-present pipe clinched between his teeth.

"What are you doing tonight?" he asked, after the niceties of greetings were beginning to wear thin.

"Oh, nothing in particular," I answered. "I'm on my way home. I had a very busy day and I'm awfully tired."

"Come, come, you're not that tired; let me take you out. I've just arrived this afternoon and you can't imagine what I've been through these past months. Summer school, after a long, tough winter, doesn't leave one with much energy. I try to limit my activities, but it never seems to work. You think you're tired! Oh, come on, let's forget about it and go out."

"I'm sorry, not tonight," I said. "Tomorrow, if you like. I'm really too fatigued to be good company."

"So am I, but I desperately need a lift," he said.

"All right, but where?" I asked.

"Never mind, I'll tell you later. What's the matter? Are you afraid to go out with me?"

"Certainly not," I said. "I would just like to know where we're going."

That settled, we walked slowly down the avenue to my home, where he chatted with my parents while I changed and off we went. After we had walked a few blocks again I asked, "Where are we going?"

"Dorothy, don't you trust me?" was all he said.

The next thing I knew, we were entering the apartment of his sister Eunice, whom I had met some years before. As we approached the living room entrance, a strange feeling of peace came over me, like a mantle of indescribable joy. It was as though a heavy weight had suddenly, with imperceptible softness, been lifted from my drooping shoulders. In its place, a calmness, never before experienced, pervaded my whole being. I knew within myself that here was the one for whom I had unconsciously waited those many, uncertain years. So overpowering was the feeling of astonishment, and awe, that I quickly sat down, involuntarily releasing a sigh of relief, as if my heart was saying, "At last."

The beauty of that first summer, filled with simple pleasures and delights of awakening love, made the season an episode of joy I would always remember. Central Park never appeared more fascinating while we sat on the grass and talked of many things. Once Alphaeus took my book of poems along, and we read to each other the sonnets of our choice. Also the enthralling evenings at Lewisohn Stadium, where one could enjoy the performances of great artists, under the warm starry skies, without the steep prices of Carnegie Hall, or the Metropolitan Opera, increased our pleasure. The summer ended far too soon. With fervent promises to write and return as soon as possible, a new chapter in our lives slowly opened and with it a stimulating friendship that was often baffling and exhausting, but above all, loving.

Our second summer brought more fun. Each experience shared added something to us, giving something more that we held in common. In that sense, the things we did were not gone and past, but lived on in us. And the thought of those pleasures, when we were separated, alleviated instead of aggravating the ache of loneliness.

"I can remember when I walked the streets for hours on end," Alphaeus wrote, "the loneliest man in the world." Every gay and happy young couple who passed him by, made him feel his loneliness more keenly and bitterly. "Now," he said, "when I go to New York, I am not alone anymore. The city is no longer the empty desert it once was, but an exciting, joyous place, all because of you."

Time passes swiftly when one is in love. Three years had elapsed since that memorable summer. Anxieties heightened; uncertainties and pressures never seemed to end. But each day our growing need for each other intensified.

Though separated from his wife, Alphaeus was not divorced. That posed a grave and urgent problem, which I thought, he seemed to be in no particular hurry to solve. Unhurried and deliberate as he was in all decisions and actions, this very important issue was no exception to the rule. It became painfully necessary to jolt him into the realization that perhaps his future would be without me. Letters came and went, thick and fast; trips to Washington and New York increased while funds decreased; nerves frayed and weeks and months slowly slipped by. Though the situation expanded my difficulties, Alphaeus's problems increased likewise, and became more exhausting due to his numerous extracurricular activities.

He was concerned about our relationship and believed he was guilty of causing me more pain than pleasure. "It isn't right," he said. "And as much as I hate to think of it — I sometimes wonder if you might not be better off in the long run, without me." He thought I needed and deserved someone who could give me more time, more attention, and more happiness.

Life for Alphaeus during those hectic years was a never-ending round of meetings, rallies, picketings and always mountains of school papers, which he often brought to New York and corrected while visiting me. The periodic escapes from the everyday routine of Washington cost him plenty in piled up work when he returned. But he didn't mind. "It was like a few bars of sweet music faintly heard through the roar and clash of daily struggle," he said.

Between the throes of personal problems, mounting school work and increased civic activities, Alphaeus at times presented a grave and gloomy picture of depression. An indefinable sadness frequently overshadowed his few fleeting joys, while the weeks dragged on relentlessly, until the next welcomed break rolled around. "Five long months to pull through now," he wrote, after spending Christmas holidays in New York. A staggering and dismal prospect for him. "Were it not for the hope and promise of the future (uncertain though it is), and your influence on me." he continued, "there would really be no point in going on with things. The thought of you, and the thought of what I **may** be able to get out of life, are the two things that keep me struggling along."

Alphaeus's outlook, on the whole, was expansive, and he continually sharpened his awareness and enlarged his scope, but, by nature, he was not very optimistic. And since he was never one to flinch at realities, and approached life, world issues in general, and problems of Blacks in particular,in a serious vein, his view of himself left him "bogged down, aimless and uncertain," with chronic fatigue dogging him at every step.

Much of his distress and despondency stemmed from an unhappy marriage, from which he tried to extricate himself with the least amount of grief to all concerned, and a host of commitments that overworked him, and scarcely left time for rest. I was eager to help lift the doldrums that clouded his outlook and dulled his spirit, and not infrequently it was possible. Yet to enter into the recesses of his innerself, one could not. Guarded by a brooding isolation, the door stood only slightly ajar, and it appeared useless to attempt to enter uninvited. "The one great problem, as I see it," he wrote during that important period, "is how to preserve one's personal independence, and at the same time live a socially effective and satisfying life." He didn't know the answer.

After another disquieting year passed, I refused to continue our relationship on the existing, unsatisfactory basis, and accused Alphaeus of lack of positiveness in his personal affairs and trying to avoid the subject of our future, which he denied. The truth of the matter was a deep-seated disillusionment with marriage. After two unsuccessful trials, fear gripped him when he contemplated a third. And quite consciously, he evaded the issue. Three letters are quoted in full as they were crucial at that critical period. They were the turning point in our relationship. One I wrote, but, because of many changes it was rewritten, and the original I kept with his letters.

Dearest, I received your letter yesterday. I must confess that it gave me something of a surprise. You have never said or written anything like that before. All evening and this morning I have been thinking of the things you said.

Your letter is not easy to answer. As you know, I am a very reserved and undemonstrative person in personal matters and consequently, I am afraid anything I may say may seem cold and void of feeling, when compared with your letter, and you may misunderstand this as a rebuke, **Please** don't think that. I must risk such misinterpretation however, in saying what I honestly feel - which I know is what you want me to do.

First of all, let me answer your request that I tell you that I feel as you do about our relationship. You say that I have won your love and possess your heart completely - something that occupies the center of one's existence, not momentarily, but as a constant something. Is that right? And is that your feeling? I mean, not simply now when there is the pain of parting, but as a continuing thing.

If you are asking me if I feel that, then darling —even though it may hurt us both to say so - I must say no. I don't believe that I am capable of having such a feeling for anyone. I do not mean that you do not fill a very important place in my life - you do, and when I am with you, there are moments when I feel that my existence is complete, my contentment perfect! but they are only moments - fleeting: my mind will not stay quiet and at peace, it goes off laboring upon this or that problem which I have been working on and to which I must return. I may want to escape from the work at times, and I want to do so desperately. But I cannot escape completely. Even when I am with you, as I have said, my mind restlessly continues to labor on. My work, then (and of course I don't mean merely my school work) appears to occupy the central place of my life.

Perhaps it should be otherwise, I don't know. Perhaps my personality is twisted in some way. I truly believe that human companionship is the most necessary and vital thing in the world, but it is not the only necessary and vital thing in my opinion.

You are preciously dear to me, no one else has given my life so much brightness and joy. I know that I can trust in you absolutely. And I love you for all your splendid qualities as a woman and a human being. I mean all these things truly.

But the responsibility which you place upon me when you say that I hold your heart in the palm of my hand is a heavy one. And being the kind of person I am, I am not sure whether I can successfully shoulder the responsibility. A person who cannot give all of himself to another has no right, has no business asking all of another. I did not consciously endeavor to make you love me - I don't suppose that's possible in any case; but I probably haven't consciously made sufficient effort to prevent you from loving me. But that is equally impossible. I think - I mean it is just as difficult to stop love from growing as it is to make it grow.

I have been two hours writing this much. It took me so long because I had to clarify my own thoughts to be sure I was saying what I really meant. I don't know that I've been very successful in saying very much. You must be the judge. Tell me honestly whether the person who wrote this is the same person you thought you were giving your heart to, and whether you are willing to let that person continue possessing your heart. What ever your judgment may be, that person will continue to remain yours devotedly.

*   *   *   *   *   *   *

Darling Alphaeus, I have read your letter several times, and each time I seem to feel that you are here, by my side speaking to me softly, perhaps hesitatingly, looking at everything in the room except me (but I don't mind) and telling me honestly how you feel. I look at you, and smile, for I seem to know exactly how your mind works, and I am not surprised as you utter your words.

I had no idea, darling, that my letter would cause you undue alarm. Perhaps I should have restrained my emotions a bit, and not have said so much, but if I cannot feel free with you, with whom then shall it be? I am so unlike you in that respect. Although I probably have never said or written as much before, for the simple reason I've never felt this way before. Neither did I think I was saying anything that you did not already know.

Your letter has not been misunderstood dear, because, much that you wrote, I was aware of, long, long ago. You see, I made it my business to study you, your likes and dislikes, as best I could; and I've tried to understand the way you think; to analyze your various views on certain points, in order to know the real you, and not merely the one on the surface. I can't say that I have been very successful, for that takes years of sincere effort and under closer contact. But I do believe I have gained a better knowledge of the big (I), fairly well, and for that, I'm proud.

Strange as it may seem, I do understand love exactly as you do - on some points, yes; but my interpretation is somewhat different. When I said that you had won my heart and held it in the palm of your hand, I really meant just that; but I'm quite sure I did not say you **possessed** it, which is a different matter. To me that word is misleading in this instance, because I always associate it with ownership, and I definitely did not mean that. I shall always love you dear, come what may, and I'm not afraid to admit it. Love is a vital part of my life, as it should be in everyone's life.

One characteristic of **real** love is, I believe, as you say, all consuming. But only in the sense that it consumes all the pettiness, selfishness, jealousy, hate, pride and the numerous other nasty faults each has. In fact it burns up all the excess baggage we have been carrying around for years, causing endless troubles. When this fire (as I term it) starts burning, everything goes that stands in the way of **true** love; and we awake to find the flowers of passion have been burnt away, and only the **true** remains. It then burns slowly, but beautifully, with a light blue flame, no longer a flaming red, fluttering and wavering as before; but with a warm, soft glow that gives comfort and light, evenly and without effort. This is my understanding of love as all consuming - leaving the nature more purified and noble than before.

I don't believe one's love for another should occupy the center of one's existence - frankly, that to me would be stagnation, and stagnation is death. Though a basic necessity, and without it in some degree life is empty and meaningless; it can only become a constant force that flows along undisturbed by the occasional rough spots, when it's real.

Dear darling Alphaeus, I understand you perfectly. Of course you haven't **that** kind of love you described for me. I would not want it either - what a drab useless life that would be. No two people are entirely sufficient unto each other that their interest in life begins and ends with each other. Such possessive love is not real. To enjoy, cherish, respect, love and adore, but **never** possess -this is real - always must one be free. You used possessed in your letter twice, dear - I think you misquoted me.

39

Who am I, that I should be the center of your existence? I do want your companionship, affection and kindness, because I feel the need of the help which can come only from the complement of myself. But I do not want it, if I am unable in return to stimulate your noblest aspirations and help spur you on to greater heights in your chosen field of work. I would be unworthy as a woman to take from you what my being needed, if I could not give to you what yours needed. Only in so doing can the greatest good be achieved by both.

I know where your heart is. It's where your mind is, and your mind is seldom off your work. That, and only that is the center of your life, and I think that is where it should be. If someone should try to make it otherwise, you might try to comply, just to please, but in the end, you would be most unhappy and quite miserable. Of course you need to escape from the bonds of labor, at times. We all do; one must play as well as work.

Darling, is being the recipient of my love such a heavy burden? That is far from what I want it to be. I love you dear, not in spite of what you are, but because you are what you are. Not because I want you for myself, alone, but because you give so much of yourself for others, who need you more than I. Neither do I expect you to be as I. You are very different in many ways; yet it is probably these differences which drew us closer. What ever it is I shall always be grateful for the happiness that has been mine, through knowing you.

You spoke of a person nor being able to give all of himself to another - not having the right to ask all of another. That depends! Suppose one wants to give all; can't help but give all, finds joy in giving all; yet neither requires or wants all from another. Yet both are happy in the amount that each exchanges; both are doing what each has to do. The proportions of giving may not be equal, but each one's need is met. You see, some of us may not need the same amount, neither can each of us give the same amount. One can only do what one is capable of, forgetting who gives more or less. That is unimportant if the needs of each are fulfilled.

This has been a difficult letter to write, but I hope it will give you a better understanding of me. Dear Alphaeus, you are still the same person I gave my patched up heart to, willingly and sincerely, not because of some fleeting whim, but because a force greater than I drew it there. And now that it has found its long sought resting place; it is perfectly content to remain there, only if doing so, it can bring joy and happiness to the house in which it rests. Be at peace darling, the storm will pass, and I will always be your Dorothy.

*   *   *   *   *   *   *

Dearest: I cannot begin to tell you with what joy and wonder I read your letter, [Alphaeus wrote several days later.] ...wonder at your deep understanding of life in general and of me in particular, and joy in the fact that our views of this thing called love coincided and agreed so perfectly.

My anxiety about how you would react to my letter proves how much I need to keep your love - but it also proves that I haven't been properly attentive enough to realize fully the kind of love it was. I had forgotten the times we had talked about love and how you had repeatedly said, that love must be unselfish, must not try to possess, and I was not thinking of the numerous little ways in which you have demonstrated this in your relationship with me.

You say you seemed to know in advance what I was going to say. Which means that you were aware of how little I knew the true you. You were aware of this but still did not become impatient with my blindness. I can't forgive myself for being so stupid. And I am ashamed of the comparison with your wisdom and generous understanding. You are a wonderful person, truly. I agree with every sentence and every word in your letter.

Love as a mutual exchange, freely given, is not a responsibility (except in so far as we cherish anything that is dear to us), but a joy. As it has always been a joy to have your warm and tender regard. And I most certainly do want to remain the recipient of that affection and regard.

Alphaeus thought he might be free the following summer, but he couldn't guarantee it.

> If you do believe in my desire to put our relationship on a sounder and more satisfactory basis at the earliest possible moment, I know you will be patient. When I think of you, I think of a soothing peacefulness more than anything else. It is that which gives me strength and joy. That is the last thing on earth I wish to destroy. Yet that is just what I am or was guilty of. Forgive me.The first and last commandment is that we must each always — **always**— be a source of strength and joy to each other, come what may. Good night, my dearest, I embrace you with all my heart.

When Alphaeus's father was in Japan, he wrote in his much used notebook the precepts of Iyeyasu, translated by Professor K. Wadagaki. He read them often and repeated them to his wife when she became impatient. I, in turn, during those doubtful years was many times in need of such excellent advice, and agreed with him that:

> Life is like unto a long journey with a heavy load. Let thy steps be slow and steady, that thou stumble not. Persuade thyself that imperfections and inconvenience is the natural lot of man, and there will be no room for discontent, neither for despair.

> When ambitious desires arise in your heart, recall the days of extremity thou hast passed through. Forebearance is the root of quietness and assurance forever. Look upon wrath as thine enemy. If thou knowest only what it is to conquer, and knowest not what it is to be defeated, woe unto thee! It will fare ill with thee. Find fault with thyself rather than others. Better less than the more.

The spring of 1943, though bleak and cold at the outset, bringing snow flurries and gusty winds instead of the beauties of the fragrant cherry blossoms, warming to the oncoming sun, was nevertheless Spring in all its glory to Alphaeus and me. Quietly, and unknown to anyone except mother and a dear friend with whom I lived, we slipped over to Alexandria, Virginia, that cold Easter Saturday and took our vows, though they had long ago been exchanged in the temple of our hearts.

Plans had been completed for Alphaeus to join the staff of the Council on African Affairs, in New York, as Educational Director. It was a challenging opportunity, and he felt his abilities and interest would be better served in the kind of work outlined by Dr. Max Yergan, its chairman. The research involved especially attracted him. He was eager to leave Washington and the confining classrooms of Howard University which increasingly seemed to stifle his expanding spirit; and he decided to resign immediately had his request for a year's leave of absence been denied. That, however, was not necessary, and in mid-July 1943, Alphaeus moved to New York.

True to his dedication, he plunged into his new occupation with zest and enthusiasm, spurred on by the prospects of implementing new and vital channels of communication that would give assistance to the African struggles. My role as wife and companion brought much pleasure, but it was obvious that adjustments on my part were indispensable if there was any hope of our marriage succeeding, and I intended to do my utmost to make it succeed. Living daily under the same roof provides a fertile field for better understanding of one another. The shades and lights visible on the picture at a distance, and perhaps seem through a dark, misty lens, now reveal themselves in all varied, subtle colors. Some never discerned before.

Naturally modest, retiring, and somewhat shy, Alphaeus had a strong need for companionship; he showed his love through kindness, rather than outward displays of affection, and was loyal and devoted in his peculiar way. Yet, as the months slipped by, it became extremely difficult to adapt to his habitually silent manner, a trait that annoyed me, at times, to utter exasperation, and which I tried to help him overcome by frequently prying for information, that was rarely offered on his own initiative. I soon learned to live with it, however, for I knew that merely my presence in the room while he worked was all he needed. Home conveyed to him an oasis of quietness in a strife-torn world, where he found freedom for a while from a stressful job.

Though never demanding, Alphaeus always wanted me around when he was home, and I often sat with him for two hours while he worked without exchanging a single word. Yet, we felt in perfect sympathy. But he never failed to turn around if I got up to go our asking, "Where are you going?" The need to understand and master the knowledge of silence as well as the ability to comprehend the unspoken word, did not come easily, even though I, too, enjoyed to an extent the quiet life. Those silent, often beautiful hours, nevertheless, became a regular pattern of our lives.

We shared a wide variety of interests, particularly music and the arts; and seldom did we miss the Sunday afternoon symphonic concert on the radio.

Television never graced our home; we had little time just to sit and look. For me, my most enjoyable form of relaxation was dancing—even alone if the music was right. This was Alphaeus's "shortest suit," and to get him on the dance floor was like drilling a well, though he was thoroughly enchanted, once he started.

I frequently marveled at Alphaeus's patience and keen sense of perfection which he displayed in everything he did. No detail was too small for his attention. When we planted plugs of grass in our backyard, he insisted that the distance between each piece of sod should be measured with a ruler so that the space would be exactly as directed. The eye, which seemed quite adequate for me, was not sufficient. Occasionally, I helped with his work and received specific details on the procedure; but in the process, an easier or quicker method was sometimes found. But Alphaeus, a bit stubborn and persistent, would declare that his plan was better. Soon I learned to say nothing, but proceeded in my own way, without his knowledge, and then observed him beam with delight when I rapidly finished the job.

Gregariousnesss was not a part of his makeup, yet Alphaeus had many friends with whom he shared common mental interest, and they considered him a leader of thought and opinion in his field of activity. His analytical mind enabled him to see all sides of any question, from the other fellow's point of view as well as his own, which made him a good listener and a fair opponent, in a detached manner. Few could say that his criticism, as a rule sharp and to the point, was anything but constructive.

Our early years in the Stuyvesant section of Brooklyn were fully occupied. The Brooklyn Branch of the National Association for the Advancement of Colored People (N.A.A.C.P.), began to stir, and with it an urgent demand for action to combat the serious conditions confronting the community. Yet the need for a more progressive element within the branch was clearly apparent, if any measures would be taken to correct the badly neglected problems. Soon a core of workers emerged, and as a part of that group, we served for a number of years, helping to achieve some of the goals.

In the process, the orientation of my political understanding underwent a drastic change. My desire to acquire some knowledge of the political doctrine Alphaeus espoused and the social belief that had become his way of life, led me to take courses at the Jefferson School of Social Science. Alphaeus taught Democratic Tradition in English Literature, and was a Trustee. For the first time, I was exposed to Marxist philosophy. A completely materialistic approach to man and life, however, ran counter to my convictions and beliefs and was therefore unacceptable; yet there were various aspects of the Science of Society with which I wholeheartedly agreed.

Before our marriage, we had many stimulating and at times heated (on my part) discussions on politics and religion. My knowledge of politics and the science of society was practically nil. Like so many of my generation, I was politically unconscious. Attendence at the Young Democratic League did not enhance my concern, and my political activities remained minimal. Our family was conservative, Republican, as far as father's views were concerned (and he ruled the house); politics was not an earnest interest of mine. Mother, a very religious woman, became a pillar of the Presbyterian Church and served for years as a deaconess, while father, a Mason, whose criticism of the intolerance and bigotry of organized religion never ceased, went to church only at Easter, and then under pressure. Yet, he insisted that my two sisters and I attend Sunday School. Teaching Sunday School, for more years than I can remember, became a part of life. Religion was always basic to my nature, though I left the church years before meeting Alphaeus.

For a long time I diligently searched for answers to many perplexing questions about life, questions that had plagued me since my youth, and had become increasingly persistent. Who am I? Where did I come from? Where am I going? What is the real purpose of life? These were profound subjects, the explanations of which seemed to have gotten lost through the maze of creeds, dogmas, and the rituals of the institution of theology. Convincing interpretations of those gnawing queries, the religion I had been taught could not answer. To satisfy that longing for a more lucid and acceptable philosophy of life, and find adequate answers to some of those disturbing questions, my quest took me far afield, through various concepts of religious and philosophical thought, until I eventually found that portion of Truth that was meaningful to me and gave me a deeper understanding of life as I saw it.

As a Marxist scholar, Alphaeus naturally disagreed with my philosophy. We always maintained a healthy respect for each other's views, and finally realized the uselessness of further discussions on the topic. It was better to let sleeping dogs lie, and build our future on the mutual aspects of our companionship, that were sufficient to withstand the thrust of a changing world.

Alphaeus firmly believed that one should understand one's society first, before one could really understand oneself and others. A view I did not share. Understanding oneself came first, to me. Though it required sensitiveness of feeling, patient insight and unselfish curiosity — qualities which do not thrive so well in this day of machines, speed, hard facts and struggle for survival, nevertheless, I continued to argue my point. In the end, Alphaeus said he sometimes felt with the poet Matthew Arnold:

> weary of myself and sick of asking
> what I am and what I ought to be,

But he never found the conclusions which he arrived at —

Resolve to be myself; and know that he,
who finds himself, loses his misery!

Those solutions he found satisfactory for his own ponderings.

---

4. THE NATIONAL NEGRO CONGRESS

At the turn of the century, the United States had become the leading manufacturing country in the world, and by 1929 was securely entrenched in first place in practically every other field as well. The giant corporations, enjoying advantages of unlimited power, made possible by lack of government control and favoritism from the Supreme Court, gradually penetrated nearly every corner of the globe, and not always by peaceful means. By 1920, the rising economy had reached its peak, but the devastating Wall Street crash of 1929 brought the country to economic paralysis. Bread lines were everywhere. The terrifying depression, the likes of which the country had never known, spread across the land. Banks closed, and millions roamed the streets in search of jobs that did not exist. The economy of the richest country in the world collapsed, and by 1932, reached its nadir. Blacks, as usual, struggling to get a foothold in the last rung of the slippery economic ladder, found themselves, not unexpectedly, at an "all time low" on the living scale.

Brought face to face with the stark, disturbing realities of the dehumanizing conditions in the slums of Washington, where many Blacks were compelled to live, Alphaeus's sensitive nature rebelled against the rampant exploitation and oppression that grimly held them, as in a vise; and shortly after his arrival at Howard, he became involved in a number of Civil Rights programs.

During the precarious years of the thirties, when the prevailing state of racial discrimination was at its height, the clamor for equality and justice became louder and stronger, giving birth to the National Negro Congress. The Congress held its first meeting in Chicago on February 14, 15, and 16, 1936, with John P. Davis National Secretary, and A. Philip Randolph, organizer of the Brotherhood of Sleeping Car Porters, its first president. The N.N.C., as it was called, met to explore ways and means of eliminating the intensified difficulties facing Blacks, which had become increasingly unbearable with the passage of time.

The Congress was well attended with 817 delegates presenting their credentials from 585 organizations, and several hundred visitors and official observers. The general sessions, held at night, showed the deep concern of more than five thousand persons at each meeting who braved the bitter cold and icy streets to lend their support to the fighting program of the Congress.

One of the major points stressed was the necessity of joint action by Blacks themselves, but cooperation with friendly organizations of other races was also required to solve the intensified economic dilemma facing all citizens. They aimed to enlist all trade unions, fraternal organizations, religious and civic groups, and all others interested in a united campaign to win for the people complete economic, cultural, political and social equality. To that end, the N.N.C. became a federation of nearly 3,000 affiliated groups of various types, banded together in a militant struggle against intolerance, discrimination, and grievances wherever found.

Alphaeus was a member of the National Executive Board; he helped to organize the Washington Council, and was Vice President. As chairman of the Labor Committee, he worked untiringly to bring Black workers into the trade unions, and assisted them in their day to day conflicts for better wages, job security and improved working conditions.

Blast Jim Crow Out of Washington was the caption of a colorful leaflet in bold, blaring letters, he prepared for the campaign to build the N.N.C. "Washington sets the pattern of discrimination against the Negro people," he wrote. "The nation's laws are made in Washington, and establish the nation's unwritten laws by unofficial endorsement of, or passive indifference to practices of discrimination, segregation and brutal oppression against the Negro people in the nation's capital."

The N.N.C. waged a constant campaign to break down the barriers preventing Black clerical and skilled workers in both government and non-government jobs. In the District Building clerkship was barred, as well as in the telephone, gas, electric and street car companies. Even chain stores followed that heinous pattern. Yet, the Black population contributed a large share of the income of public utilities and chain stores.

"I've just been on a delegation to the management of a chain store," Alphaeus wrote, "to demand employment of Negro clerks in one of the new stores opening tomorrow in a Negro neighborhood." The company employed Blacks only as porters and laborers in its twenty odd stores in the city. "Despite an hour and a half of threats of picketing and boycott on the part of all Negroes in the community," he continued, "the management refused to budge a **half-inch.**"

The Labor Committee, always swamped with pressing situations, had a particularly serious one with the lengthy hotel strike. Half of more than two thousand workers out of the 63 hotels on strike were Blacks. Alphaeus was painfully disturbed by lack of concern of many who could and should have given their support to the issue. "While Washington colored folks are all greatly excited about the Marian Anderson case (and rightly so)," he informed me, "there has been hardly a ripple of interest in this much more important matter." To make the condition worse, some Howard students took jobs as scabs. Since the University officials would do nothing to punish the students; only strong expression on the campus could deter them. Alphaeus, as chairman of the committee, had his hands full trying to stop the Black scabs, and get more Blacks on the picket line.

The picture of repression in the nation's capital was typical of most of the states and presented a repugnant and offensive scene. In some theatres and many restaurants admission was denied; and though Blacks were a third of the population, there were none in the Health, Tax, or other civil divisions of the District of Columbia government.

Schools and playgrounds fell far below the needs of the community, forcing thousands of youngsters to play on the dangerous streets, which resulted in the injury of 1,138 children in one year and eight killed. The city had adequate funds to maintain modern golf courses, tennis courts for night playing, polo fields and other elaborate recreational facilities barred to Blacks but supported by their money as taxpayers.

The N.N.C. mobilized action to rectify that serious grievance. Alphaeus wrote a scathing bulletin with facts collected on the manner in which Black children were being victimized by systematic discrimination in Federal appropriations for teachers and buildings. The result of that militant campaign won important gains for the schools and complete reorganization of the recreation program that included Black administrative and supervisory officials in the new setup, for the first time.

From the outset of our friendship, a perfectly clear picture of Alphaeus's deep involvement in the immense racial problems confronting the nation emerged through his letters, which often contained material he had written, and rarely omitted some reference to the varied activities that absorbed so much of his time. He was wholly committed, (without reservation) to the total freedom of Black Americans, and though he repeatedly made glowing promises to take on less and less assignments, he was never able to keep one.

"What a week!" he wrote. "Now that the weekend meeting of the American Congress for Peace and Democracy, the special meeting of the Negro people on the lifting of the Spanish Embargo and the banquet in honor of Dr. Donawa (do you know him - he served eighteen months in the medical service in Spain), and the monthly meeting of the Howard Teacher's Union — now that all these things in the past six days are over, I have a little breathing spell to put myself together and pay some attention to you." Few hours were left to pay much attention to me. Alphaeus's keen sense of responsibility and humaneness, which would not permit him to give less than his best, taxed his capacity to the utmost, and seldom could he find time to take heed to personal matters. "Another one of those mad scramble days," was the opening sentence of one letter, "winding up at the Post Office with a heap of mail (sample enclosed) at this hour, (12:45 A.M.) when I should be in bed." The enclosed sample was a leaflet he wrote. **Make the District Budget Serve the Human Needs of the Community.** Typical of the Black community, it was in dire need of many utilities. To keep them better informed, and to be certain they understood what was happening to the funds allocated to the District, Alphaeus interpreted the budget issue's effects on Blacks and pointed out effective lines of action.

Young volunteers worked the old clanking mimeograph machine in the crowded, busy office hours overtime, more often than not, and frequently late into the night. As no one in the Washington Council was paid, workers gave their time when it could be spared. That meant a few core people shouldered the responsibility of seeing that the basic tasks were accomplished. Alphaeus played a key role. Aside from the grueling occupation with the Labor Committee, which never had a dearth of urgent issues; he headed delegations, edited news letters, wrote bulletins and prepared leaflets, many times under pressure at the last minute. "He generally worked quietly, sensing and doing what needed to be done, seldom making the big speeches, and never seeking the headlines; but those of us who worked with him knew very well that he was the mainstay of the struggle.''[1]

The preparation for the third N.N.C. conference held in Washington, April 1940, had filled Alphaeus's mind and time for weeks, and was a long hard drive; but he felt the results were well worth the strain. His participation was mainly behind-the-scenes work; seeing that things ran smoothly, and taking charge of registering 1,300 delegates from 29 states and Haiti, which the staff continued to count until 4 A.M., and again the following night. In the committee assigned to draw up a national constitution, he had considerable trouble, as chairman, trying to smooth out differences of opinion before reaching the final draft. Agreement was finally attained and unanimously accepted by the Congress.

The culmination of all the activities that kept Alphaeus constantly on his toes was the last minute call to substitute for Max Yergan in giving a radio address, **Negroes and the War,** which had a nationwide hookup.

In the field of Health and Housing — accommodations were shockingly inferior, especially in the sphere of tuberculosis hospitalization. Disease infested slums, tenanted by poor Black families in Jim-Crow Washington were legion. It was not hard to understand why 22 out of every thousand Blacks died each year, compared to 13.4 white persons for each thousand. The N.N.C. tackled that situation from several angles: Health and housing conferences were sponsored; 40,000 health education pamphlets were distributed to school children; and a city-wide survey was diligently conducted and the results submitted to the White House.

Police brutality grew particularly vicious during those years. Hundreds of Black boys were arrested every month — held for investigation as vagrants, often brutalized and beaten in police stations. The N.N.C. through its Civic Affairs Committee, headed by Dr. Doxey A. Wilkerson, nationally known educator, as chairman, took the lead in the drive which exposed and checked the long series of insults, abuses, and "urban lynchings," and battled throughout its existence to put an end to police terror.

Apart from the urgency of compelling problems that confronted the Council from day to day, the stress of not having sufficient funds to carry forward the work from month to month never lifted. Fund raising, a vital function of the movement, consumed much time and energy; and Alphaeus, with his keen organizational ability, worked out many campaigns to keep the crusade afloat.

"Thank God, that job is over." he wrote, after three weeks of hard labor with the committee. "The dinner last night was a success, despite a torrential rain." The guests overwhelmed Alphaeus with their congratulations. The slipshod manner in which articles were checked marred the total effect, and the job fell to him to straighten out hats, coats, rubbers and umbrellas, so that there would be no scandal of stolen mink coats. When it was all over, two good, stiff drinks helped to ease his tension.

At the height of the deep depression, in the mid-thirties when the New Deal attempted to repair the catastrophic damages of the 1929 crash, the largest public works program ever undertaken by this government was launched, The Works Progress Administration (W.P.A.). Throughout the country tremendous construction took place, and gradually the population began to take a new lease on life, which good honest labor can create. The well-being of Blacks, however, seemed not to be in the recovery plan, and it was necessary for N.N.C. delegates to go before the W.P.A. officials and District Commissioners to demand the enlargement of the wholly insufficient work and relief benefits for thousands of unemployed Blacks in the city.

The situation was extremely grave. Representatives and delegations from various groups, acting jointly as the **Citizens Conference on Jobs and Welfare** with Alphaeus as the leader, presented a five-point program to the Commissioner, December 1941, which included among other recommendations, a lifting of the $60-a-month "Relief Ceiling" which imposed serious hardships on the impoverished persons in large families, and a broadening of the 5 cent milk plan to include all persons on W.P.A. The struggle was long and heated, but continued unabated in spite of setbacks, until they realized significant gains.

The predicament was equally frustrating with the Unemployment Compensation Commission, which refused to consider the appointment of ·qualified Black claims examiners, but persistent pressure by the Council forced the Commissioner to reconsider; and three Black examiners were appointed.

The problems the N.N.C. faced seemed endless, and the magnitude of the task often overpowering. Despite President Roosevelt's order — discrimination in government employment continued unheeded and remained an established practice for lack of a Civil Rights Bill. Delegations conferred with the Fair Employment Practices Committee (F.E.P.C.); picket lines supported laundry workers fighting for collective bargaining rights; and masses demonstrated for employment of Blacks in the Capital Transit Company, that was frantically advertising for new men, even up to the age of 55, but stubbornly refused to hire a single Black. Alphaeus, you may be sure, was in the thick of all those drives.

With the intensified World War II emergency, however, the need to train Black workers for skilled jobs was raised to a new level of importance. In calling for "all-out defense of democracy," and at the same time tolerating the exclusion of Blacks in defense industries, the federal officials were in a totally untenable position. The N.N.C. was determined to break the deadlock, particularly in the Glen L. Martin Aircraft Plant, Baltimore, Maryland, which had huge government defense contracts, but consistently denied employment to Blacks, except in a menial capacity. As chairman of the "Jobs Campaign" Alphaeus spearheaded that fight for "all-out defense of democracy" in defense industry — right here at home. The drive brought the charge from the Dies Committee on Un-American Activities, that the campaign for jobs for Blacks at the Glen Martin Aircraft factory sought to "sabotage" defense production through "infiltration" of Black communist workers. The Congress immediately called the charge a "vicious slander against the Negro people," and urged all Blacks to renew their fight for work in defense industries.

Not only did the Dies Committee attack the Congress as sponsors of the campaign, it also branded Alphaeus a communist because of his activities on behalf of the American Peace Mobilization. Alphaeus issued the following statement through the office of the N.N.C. on May 22, 1941:

> The Negro people have long been asking why the Dies Committee does not devote one-tenth of its time to investigating the subversive undermining of American democracy represented by the varied forms of discrimination and oppression practiced against Negro citizens — especially flagrant now is the denial of jobs to Negroes in certain defense industries. Mr. Dies and his committee notwithstanding, I believe in democratic rights for all citizens, regardless of race color or creed, and I shall continue to work for these

rights. And I am not a communist any more than are millions of other Americans who believe in the same thing.

I have participated in the work of the American Peace Movement, an organization national in scope, which is dedicated to the maintenance of peace and democracy in America. I see nothing subversive in that. You cannot make something bad by merely calling it a name.

I knew absolutely nothing about the charges against me prior to reading about them in the newspaper of May 21, and I was not called in to testify at the hearing. This is merely another instance of the reprehensible practice of the Dies Committee, condemned time and again by high officials, of accepting and publicizing any slanderous testimony without making the slightest effort to corroborate the facts.

The same day Alphaeus sent a telegram to the Dies Committee, which read:

As an American citizen I demand the right to testify before your committee and face the investigator who made the charges of communism against me and protest failure of your committee to notify me of charges and secure my appearance.

November 10, 1942, Alphaeus received a letter from the Federal Security Agency:

Dear Mr. Hunton:

The Federal Bureau of Investigation recently sent us a report concerning you.

The Subversive Personnel Committee of the Federal Security Agency has reviewed the contents of their report and is glad to be able to notify you that we have found notning in the report showing that you have engaged in any activities which might properly be characterized subversive or disloyal to our government. You have therefore been exonerated and the Federal Bureau of Investigation has been so notified.
Very truly yours,

Arthur B. McLlean
Acting Director of Personnel

Alphaeus was disturbed by the fact that Washington was not pressing for the opening of the Second Front at a crucial point in World War II. The delay compelled him and others to work unstintingly to make a success of the N.N.C. sponsored rally to dramatize the issue in the fall of 1942. He also became very active in the peace movement in the fall of 1942. The attitude of many Blacks, who did not, or could not understand the nature of the conflict brutally waged in Europe was for him a source of acute irritation and regret.

His mother arrived for a short visit, soon after the meeting, and Alphaeus accompanied her on social calls. "One thing I got from being with her friends," he wrote, "was a better understanding of how some Negroes, (the better off middle-class Negroes) feel about the war. They want Japan to win." The viewpoints they expressed shocked him. Some thought Japan was justified in kicking the "white man" out of China and exploiting the Chinese themselves. They didn't see any difference between World War II and the last, and quoted all the anti-administration opinions that they read in the Hearst and other appeasement papers. Without allowing himself to get angry or to argue, Alphaeus tried to point out a few simple facts about the war, which should have cleared away some of their false ideas. He might as well have kept silent, for all the good it did. "If only there was some way of forcing these people to read progressive news regularly for one month," he said. "I don't know what else will change them unless, perhaps a bomb or two dropped on their heads from a Japanese plane. Ignorance — and especially among supposedly educated people, is a damnable thing."

In an article in "Today's Guest Column" of the **People's Voice**, Alphaeus wrote two years later in this same vein, entitled "Negro People Concerned with Africa's Future."

> Although the American Negro, as we said in this column last week, rejects as an insult the "Back to Africa" mouthings of a Bilbo or a Gerald K. Smith, that does not mean he is indifferent to the future of Africa and its people...

> All of this, of course, simply means that the Negro is keenly aware of the stakes of freedom in this war. Along with the higher level reached among the Negro people in their struggle for full rights in this country, there has developed a closer relationship to the struggles of other oppressed peoples...

> There is, however, one dangerous element still too often noticeable in the Negro's thinking about the darker peoples of the world. It is the tendency to view the problem as one of conflict between darker-skinned

people **in general** and white people **in general**. This is
the basis of the racial separatism advocated by Marcus
Garvey and by the surviving remnants of his followers
today. This is the basis of a George S. Schuyler's
cynical defeatism and his argument for a long war as
aiding the Negro's cause. Likewise, it is the basis of
some recent prophecies of a third World War between
the races.

The National Negro Congress has consistently
championed the solidarity of Negro and white labor.
The National Association for the Advancement of
Colored People at its recent convention in Chicago
gave convincing expression to this principle. These
and other Negro organizations and interracial bodies,
together with organized labor, must increase their
efforts toward promoting clarity of thinking among
both Negro and white Americans with respect to racial
issues, not only in domestic affairs but in international
affairs.

All enemies of the United Nations know that in narrow racial nationalism they have a fertile field in
which to sow their seeds of division and discord...

The influence of the defeatist forces among the
Negro people and among white workers must be
nullified by driving home in graphic and inescapable
terms the realization that no nation or group of people
can find security and democracy today outside the
framework of world-wide security and democracy in
which all groups and nations work together for their
mutual benefit.

The idea of a separatist "Back to Africa" movement is a reactionary pipe-dream, opposed to the objectives of the United Nations and opposed to the
determination of the Negro people to win full
democratic rights in this country to which they owe
allegiance. Just as the struggle here will be won
through the collaboration and unity of the progressive
forces in every section of the population, so the liberation and progress of the African people and other colonial subjects must come through the concerted efforts of the United Nations, first, in winning a decisive
victory over fascism and second, in building a new
world of equality, justice and peace. The darker

peoples in every land have helped in the winning of the
war, and their full cooperation on a democratic basis
will be essential in the winning of the peace.

With the resignation of John P. Davis, the National Secretary of the
N.N.C. in January 1943, the National office from which the Washington
Council worked, closed, though it continued to function full speed in New
York. Lack of office space and a secretary, however, made the task of car-
rying on the Council work extremely difficult and much of a burden on
Alphaeus. He had at that time the main, arduous responsibility of trying
to round up 75-100 delegates to attend the conference in New York in
April, and the added chore of assisting in raising funds for their railroad
fare by means of a party.

In New York, Alphaeus took on a new job with the Council on African
Affairs. Despite the heavy load, he continued to work in the N.N.C.,
though mainly as a member of the National Executive Board, and the
Editorial Board of the **Congress View,** a monthly bulletin, published by
the New York Council, which provided a "house organ" for the Councils
and friends of the Congress, and attempted to reflect correctly and
faithfully the most urgent desires of the Black people.

After eleven years of consistent struggle and effective work in numerous
areas of struggle, with productive National conferences and 50 branch
Councils in 19 States, the beleaguered and harassed Congress was forced
to disband, thus becoming another victim of the atrocious red-baiting of a
frightened government. The strife was long; the conflicts intense; there
were failures to be sure, and the victories were hard to win; but, because
the National Negro Congress existed, significant progress was made in the
cause of racial justice.

5. THE COUNCIL ON AFRICAN AFFAIRS (PART I)

The white invaders' first measure of Africa's wealth was its men, women and children, whom they bought with a few trinkets or seized at gun point. The human bounty, in chains, was then sold in the open market as slaves. Later, the rapacious European trading companies measured African wealth in gold, diamonds, and ivory, and built immense overseas empires that made no end of money for the financier and wealthy country gentlemen back home. Today, Africa's wealth is measured in mineral ores and raw materials for industry and armament.

The last continental stronghold of colonialism, where the crumbling system of colonial imperialism prevailed after World War II, Africa became a key area in international, political, and economic affairs. As far as many people knew then, it could just as well have been on the other side of Mars. It was even more difficult for most to realize the enormous size of the African continent, which can hold very comfortably the United States, India and China with plenty of room to spare.

To combat that appalling ignorance, a small group of concerned people met at 8 West 40th Street, New York City on January 28, 1937, and formed the **International Committee on African Affairs.** Among the twelve founding members was one of the great singers of our time, Paul Robeson, a dedicated fighter in the cause of human dignity and world peace, who became the chairman, and served in that capacity for eighteen years, until the organization was forced to disband.

"If Africa is not today in the headlines, it does not mean that life there has ceased to be full of tragic problems," read the committee's announcement of its first affair at the International House, on September 7th. "There is a real sense in which Africa's ills have become chronic..." the notice continued. "The ruthless exploitation of the people; repressive legislation of the most destructive type, and the growing poverty of the Africans."

One of the purposes of the International Committee on African Affairs was to inform public opinion on what was happening to and in Africa. They were fortunate to have in America, for a brief period, two Africans eminently qualified to speak on the inside facts of the political and economic affairs of Africa. They were, Professor D.D.T. Jabavu, who was connected with the South African Native College at Fort Hare, South Africa, and President of the All African Convention, and Dr. Alfred Xuma, a practicing physician at Johannesburg and Vice-President of the All African Convention.

News of Africa, the committee's first publication, a two page news letter edited by Freida Neugelbauer, appeared in August 1942. At that time, India represented a decisive factor in the colonial world, and a very explosive situation continued to slowly brew in that vast country. At the same time, India's stalwart leader and statesman, Jawaharlal Nehru, languished in prison because of his demand for a Free India — free from the domination of British rule.

The Council on African Affairs, the group's new name, took up the challenge and held a mass meeting on the **Crisis in India — Its Relation to the Colonial World,** at Manhattan Center, where 4,000 people cheered enthusiastically when Kumar Goshal, the noted Indian author, cried, "Give India a National government."

To be associated with the Council pleased Alphaeus. He realized the necessity of the important work to promote the African peoples' welfare and to develop a better understanding among Americans. He also recognized the need to clarify Africa's place in that global peoples' war and in the global peace to follow, particularly among Blacks, organized labor and progressive groups.

"Just as labor and the liberal forces of England recognized 180 years ago that their own interest lay in the overthrow of American slavery," he told an interviewer on his first day at the office in the summer of 1943, "so today it is necessary for Americans and all peoples of the anti-axis world to realize that their future security and peace must ultimately depend upon the abolition of the principle and practice of imperialism in Africa and throughout the world."

As Educational Director, Alphaeus had hopes of mobilizing public support for the Council by developing a program upon a systematic and mass appeal basis; a program that would influence mass opinion and action, and justify the Council's existence, or it would cease to exist. It required a great deal of research to produce his first project, the monthly bulletin, **New Africa,** a scholarly source of information and analysis of the critical problems in Africa. Of special interest was the new role of the U.S., whose colossal corporations, ever ready to take advantage of cheap labor and abundant raw materials, were investing heavily in various countries, particularly South Africa.

In early January 1944, a series of meetings sponsored by a wide range of local labor, civic and religious organizations were arranged in Montreal, Kingston, Ottawa and Toronto, Canada, dealing with the future of the peoples of Africa and other colonial areas as seen in the light of the war and the objectives of the United Nations. In Toronto, Alphaeus spoke on **"Africa — A Continent in Bondage to Imperialism,"** while Robeson addressed a mass meeting and Max Yergan, Executive Secretary, gave his talk on a coast-to-coast radio hookup.

The meetings, with their broad public auspices, were a heartening sign that the Canadians recognized the urgency of taking a stand, along with members of the British Commonwealth of nations in influencing the British colonial and foreign policies toward adherence to the terms of the Atlantic Charter to the end that all peoples in all lands may enjoy the benefits of a hard-won peace.

Since the outbreak of World War II, the Council had advocated the general arming of Africans and the immediate removal of economic, social and political restrictions that hindered the full participation of Africa's millions and the full utilization of the continent's immense resources in the fight against fascism. The African's contribution to Allied Victory, Alphaeus pointed out in **New Africa,** was not insignificant by any means. Despite harsh, wasteful labor practices, antiquated productive methods, and barriers of every conceivable type, the campaign in North Africa, in which they played an important part, was crucial in winning the war. They had a stake in the peace, if there was to be any peace, and the Council was dedicated to their cause of freedom and justice.

To that end, Alphaeus and Yergan conferred at length with officials of the U.S. State Department's Division of African Affairs, concerning lend lease and other economic and political questions involving the U.S. Government, Ethiopia, Liberia and other territories. Though the State Department officials reaffirmed that the United Nations' war aims applied to the people of Africa as well as all other peoples, it was doubtful if anything would be done. Pressure had to be maintained at the maximum level in order to achieve the smallest gain.

Following that discussion, Alphaeus spearheaded the Council's conference on **Africa—New Perspectives,** in New York, in April 1944, which had an attendance of nearly 200 outstanding Black and white leaders from sixty organizations. One of the distinguished participants who represented the African Students Association was Kwame Nkrumah, who later became the head of the first independent African country, Ghana, March 1957. Out of that interchange of views came a program of African postwar liberation that was endorsed by several hundred American citizens and sent to the U.S. and foreign governments. The proceedings of that conference were subsequently prepared by a committee of six (including Alphaeus) and published in a pamphlet, **For a New Africa.**

As the devastating war continued to ravage most of Europe, and violent battles raged on African soil, one Black general held North Africa as the pivot around which the French rallied when the allied fortunes in France were low and the U.S. was in peril. "No history of the African campaign can omit the name of one black man, Felix Éboué," Alphaeus wrote in the **People's Voice,** in 1945. Éboué, he pointed out "had played a key role in its successful outcome." The only African governor in the Provinces, he refused to be pressured by the surrounding governors of the French Colonies who went pro-Vichy and sought to win him over. "Éboué rallied the chiefs and tribes of the entire territory to the Allied cause and dispatched a message to General De Gaulle saying, 'as between capitulation to the enemy and prosecution of the war, we of Chad elect to war.' " By his heroic stand he made it possible for Chad to become the initial government seat in Africa for the Free French operation, which prompted the French National Committee in New York to note that "Eboue did more than any other Frenchman next to De Gaulle for the Allied cause against fascism." Soon after Éboué's death on May 17, 1944, Alphaeus wrote am inspiring article, **Éboué - A Man To Remember.**

Having assisted ably in sweeping the Axis out of their own continent, African troops were actively engaged in the cleanup in Asia. Seasoned troops from British West and East Africa, the Belgian Congo and other sections were engaged in fierce battles in Burma. One reporter stated that "Giants from the West African bush—some 6 feet 7 inches tall—were fighting the Japanese in the Arakan jungle of the Burma front." They had reached the battlefields after a march of nore than 100 miles, over mountains, across rivers and through thick bush, carrying heavy equipment and ammunition on their heads. "These troops," the reporter continued, "contributed the first major victory in Burma, annihilating a force of 8,000 Japanese, ending two weeks of hard fighting."

Among thousands of Africans who served in the army to "save the world for Democracy and the four freedoms," none of which they ever enjoyed, were the contingents of work-troops from the Union of South Africa, which did not accept African volunteers for active combat services, and for a good reason. With the mounting repressive laws governing practically every phase of their lives, South Africa would be begging for immediate trouble if a gun were places in the African's hands.

Although Alphaeus applied himself to the new tasks with his usual dedication, by mid-44, disturbing thoughts clouded his outlook regarding his work, which led him to question whether there was a satisfying future for him with the Councl, a non-profit organization, financed entirely through voluntary contributions and subscriptions to its publications. The most serious weakness on the work appeared, in his opinion, the almost total lack of discussion of general policy, of general developments in relation to Africa, and the role of the Council with regard to other forces and agencies with parallel aims.

He knew, of course, that Yergan had many heavy responsibilities besides the council. If the Council's work was important, Alphaeus expected him to allot a certain specific time to it in his regular schedule, which Yergan failed to do. It became difficult to have proper teamwork among the members of the staff, to generate interest and sufficient motivation for carrying and understanding the goals towards which the day-to-day work was directed.

Further, he believed that , without placing any undue burden on Robeson, he should be brought into such discussions where he could contribute immensely to shaping policy, and play an increasingly effective role as Chairman. In addition, Alphaeus lamented the lack of help to be secured from a regular functioning Executive Committee, that did not exist. All those things required time and effort, but the results, he felt certain, would more than compensate. As conditions stood, it was nor possible to function on a real organizational basis, and he wondered if he were not working at a dead end.

A new phase in world history had emerged, which demanded a corresponding change in the Council's work. It required a more serious approach to the role the Council should play to make it as meaningful and effective as possible in the immediate period ahead. Despite many setbacks, which rested solidly in the Executive Secretary's office, Alphaeus trudged ahead on his own initiative, doing what he thought was necessary, and assuming more and more responsibilities.

During the early years, when the C.A.A. was alone in its work, and struggling to keep alive and functioning, few people had knowledge of the highly organized culture and well integrated systems of African life prior to the European's coming. Among Blacks there was a curious division in their attitude towards their own history and progress. To many, Black did not appear beautiful. They were at once ashamed and proud; few were concerned about the strivings and desperate plight of millions of Africans. The call for assistance was a small voice crying in the wilderness. It revealed how effective the persistent efforts to instill subordination into the Black man had been by centuries of miseducation. To perpetuate the myth of racial inferiority was to the white man's economic advantage, and a massive plan for re-education was imperative if Black America were to awaken to the realization of its ties with Black Africa. A striking example of the misunderstanding and confusion surrounding the problem at that time can be seen from a young Southerner's letter.

"Dear sir, I have come upon a copy of your paper **New Africa.** I have read and re-read with fervent interest the articles contained therein. First, allow me to ask a question. Why in the world would one worry about the racial conditions in Africa when we as a minority group catch hell in this country? Chances are that I'll never make it to Africa, therefore, I'm not the least bit interested in what goes on over there, but very concerned about conditions here at home.

"I would appreciate an answer to this question and also any literature you have concerning the problems of our illustrious race, and additional information from your organization."

Alphaeus replied:

> You ask why one should worry about racial conditions in Africa, when as a minority group we catch hell in the U.S.A.? It is a question that arises frequently, although usually asked by liberal minded white people instead of Negroes.
>
> The answer is two-fold. First, we have to be concerned with the oppression of our Negro brothers in Africa for the very same reason that we here in New York or in any other state in the Union have to be concerned with the plight of our brothers in Tennessee, Mississippi or Alabama. If you say that what goes on in the United States is one thing, quite different from what goes on in the West Indies, Africa or anywhere else affecting black people, the answer is, then you are wrong. Racial oppression and exploitation have a universal pattern, and whether they occur in South Africa, Mississippi or New Jersey, they must be exposed and fought as part of a worldwide system of oppression, the fountain-head of which is today among the reactionary and fascist-minded ruling circles of white America. Jim-Crowism, colonialism and imperialism are not separate enemies, but a single enemy with different faces and different forms. If you are genuinely opposed to Jim-Crowism in America, you must be genuinely opposed to the colonial, imperialist enslavement of our brothers in other lands.
>
> Our great leaders from Frederick Douglass to Paul Robeson have emphasized and re-emphasized this lesson in both word and deed. It was Douglass' support of the Irish people's freedom struggle in his day that made it possible for Britain to rally the British workers to fight the North in the Civil War. The

workers of England took their stand on the side of
Lincoln and emancipation. This leads to the second
important part of the answer.

It is not a matter of helping the African people
achieve freedom simply out of a spirit of humanitarian concern for their welfare. It is a matter of helping the African people, because in doing so we further
the possibility of their being able to help us in our
struggles in the U.S. Can you not envision what a
powerful influence a free West Indies or a free west
Africa would be upon American Democracy? Is it not
already apparent what a difference in the world picture the birth of China has made?

Though it was difficult for some Blacks to relate to Africans in that
period, others were eager for current news and understanding of their
history, which reached back to the very dawn of human consciousness.
New Africa, later changed to **Spotlight on Africa,** tried to bridge the
gap. The circulation here and abroad increased considerably, and bulletin
news items were often quoted in African newspapers and journals. Frequently, information could not be found in any other American publication, or else it appeared weeks or months later. Among the subscribers
were a number of public and university libraries, as well as United Nations
and government representatives, anthropologists, religious leaders and
others with professional interest in Africa. It was a welcome source of
news for many.

"Had you witnessed the excitement at the distribution of the bulletin,
you would have said, 'The new day has come,'" wrote a Brooklyn junior
high school teacher. He related at length how the class was divided into
committees, and with full steam ahead went about its projects. "We know
you are a very busy man, Dr. Hunton, but if you can spare the time, we'd
love to have you tell us about **New Africa.** Can it be arranged?" It was arranged, and Alphaeus spent a gratifying hour relating some little known
facts of African history — to the eager students' delight.

Besides preparation of **Spotlight on Africa,** Alphaeus provided news
releases to sixty-two foreign papers and sixty-seven U.S. newspapers,
some as often as two or three times a week. The ever-present necessity for
consistent research on his part to keep abreast with the rapidly changing
times took the form of careful reading and digesting materials concerning
Africa, published here and abroad; newspapers, periodicals, books and
government reports from various areas in Africa, and U.N. documents
bearing on Trust territories. Additional information, which quickly
graced the printed pages of the bulletin, was derived from regular correspondence from African leaders and organizations, particularly, the

African National Congress, the largest and most powerful organization of Africans in the Union of South Africa. TheA.N.C., formed in 1912, has a long history of militant struggle for African rights, especially in leading the campaign against the much hated pass laws.

Then, there was the endless job of classifying and filing clippings, speaking engagements sandwiched between, special articles to write, and numerous information queries to answer from all sections of the country and abroad. The Council's educational services also included the maintennance of an extensive library, which Alphaeus set up. He prepared bibliographies and a fifteen page "African Bibliography" of materials published during the period from January 1945 to February 1950.

As an accredited observer at the United Nations, he reported directly and interpreted the work of the world organization in its relation to Africa. His attendance at the sessions of the Trusteeship Council, Ad Hoc Committee on Non-Self-Governing Territories, where he consulted with U.N. delegates, and prepared special memoranda for, and reports of those meetings, averaged two or three times a week.

Especially significant were trhe detailed memoranda on the South African question, when General Jan C. Smuts, Prime Minister of the Union of South Africa, came to the U.N. in 1946, to appeal for the right to annex the adjacent mandate colony of South-West Africa. Smuts no doubt put considerable reliance on the colossal ignorance that existed in the outside world, particularly in the U.S., about the real conditions in South Africa, and on his subtle play on words, aimed at the shortness of man's memories.

Alphaeus, however, had maintained close touch with developments in South Africa nd he challenged Smuts to make public the facts concerning the widespread opposition of Africans to the proposed annexation and extreme secrecy that characterized the government's investigation of opinion in South-West Africa on the issue. The Council's intervention, which was cited several times by the Indian representative, Sir Magaraj Singh, played no small part in circumventing Smut's ambitious scheme.

The real reason behind the demand for South-West Africa was, of course, the need for more cheap African labor to be exploited in the newly discovered gold mine of the Orange Free State Province, where they would immediately fall under the general body of laws that operate for all Africans in the Union of south Africa. Even greater considerations were at stake in the Smuts proposal--the fate of 350,000 Blacks in South-West Africa. There was and is no possibility of world peace unless harmony is effected between the white and colored races of the world, on the basis of racial equality.

"Ever since the conquest of South Africa, first by the Dutch and later the British, the policy of no equality both in the church and the state has become the guiding policy of successive governments," said Mr. H.A. Naidoo, leader of the Natan Indian Congress at the Council's reception for him and Dr. Alfred Xuma, President of the African National Congress, and Senator H.M. Basner, a member of the South African Parliment who represented Africans in the Transvaal and Orange Free State. The three were attending the U.N. sessions on the crutial issur of South-West Africa and were detremined to fight General Smut's blatant proposal to the bitter end. Mr. Naidoo:

> Discrimination against Africans has been justified on the grounds of trusteeship, against the Indians on the grounds that they are an alien race and as such, constitute a menace to western civilization; against the Coloreds on the grounds that they are God's step-children and therefore are incapable of being assimilated in the political life of South Africa. That this policy should be justified in the name of Christian civilization is at once an indication of the degradingly low level to which Statesmanship has sunk in South Africa.

Most of the delagates, like most ordinary people, had very little specific information on colonial conditions, andvery little time to acquire it. One of the functions of the Council was, therefore, to provide that information to the delagates as the need arose, and Alphaeus did just that. For the benefit of the members of the special **U.N. Council on Information from Non-Self-Governing Territories,** which met in September 1946, to consider the reports submitted by colonial powers, Alphaeus, with the aid of a friend, prepared a 74-page memorandum of documentated information on current conditions on Africa and other colonies. It proved very valuable to certain members of the committee in exposing the true character of colonial rule.

In connection with the General Assembly meeting, during that extremely busy year, he prepared a pamphlet, **Seeing Is Believing—The Truth About South Africa,** vividly illustrated with photographs showing the daily manifestations of discrimination and color bar enforcement. It was the third pamphlet Alphaeus had written in two years on the explosive situation on South Africa which became nore desperate each year. Ten thousand copies were printed and widely circulated here and abroad, and it was extensively quoted by some delegates during the debate on South-West Africa, and on discrimination against Indians in South Africa.

Again in the Trusteeship Council, members made use of a report Alphaeus sent them on the same issue. The questions they raised concerning conditions in South-West Africa paralleled closely, in many instances, the points set forth in his analysis. Throughout the sessions he sent weekly reports of the proceedings by air to contacts in London and Africa and kept organizations in this country likewise informed. This he did, not only for information purposes, but also to enable those contacts to make their wishes known to the U.N. as the proceedings developed and at the appropriate time prior to the decisive vote.

On the eve of the final action on the question of South-West Africa at the General Assembly in the fall of 1947, Alphaeus compiled and made public a detailed report on the oppressive conditions borne by 3000,000 Africans in that former mandated territory, which the South African government refused to bring under the U.N. Trusteeship system. The report consisted of the verbatim testimony of numerous West African tribal chiefs, headmen and other representative leaders, which Rev. Michael Scott assembled and brought to the U.N. It took Rev. Scott, a white Anglican minister, three years of persistent efforts before he was finally permitted to come before a U.N. committee. He submitted the request of the Herero and other African peoples of South-West Africa, that their chiefs be granted a hearing before the U.N., that the lands taken away from them be returned, and that South-West Africa be brought under the U,N, Trusteeship.

When Alphaeus was unable to cover the U.N. sessions, Mrs. Eslanda Goode Robeson took over as alternate observer. Mrs. Robeson, wife of the chairman, Paul Robeson, joined the staff in 1945. To her study of anthropology she had added a rich experience of direct observations of people in many countries during her wide travels in Europe, Asia and Africa, and she was the author of several books and pamphlets.

In his program, Alphaeus had confidence in the principal of "education for action," and he sought to dramatize the conditions in South Africa more descriptively by putting together, with the help of friends in the film industry, a two reel 16mm documentary sound film, **South Africa Uncensored,** a shocking revelation of oppression. The cruelty of Nazi Storm Troopers was not confined to one nationality; it was common human meanness that would burst forth anywhere. The film's scenes invariably evoked a sense of horror, and one felt limp and exhausted from sheer distress at the end. It was difficult to believe that human beings in this day and age could be subjected to such degradation.

In many respects the Council's role was in the nature of a liaison agency between the U.N. and the public, here and abroad, and particularly in Africa. The importance of that role was inestimable, because no other organization directly concerned with Africa or colonial questions in general maintained a regular observer at the United Nations' proceedings. The Council was the country's leading authority on African problems, and it sought to secure a comprehensive and effective U.N. program for the emancipation and advancement of African and Colonial peoples.

A letter from Leslie S. Perry of the National Association for the Advancement of Colored People, February 1947, gave another indication of the widespread influence of the work.

> Dear Alphaeus,
> This is just a note to congratulate you on the excellent job you did in the January 1947 issue of **New Africa** in setting forth the votes of the U.N. with respect to trusteeship agreements and other matters...As one who does not follow international affairs too closely, I was certainly dismayed to find that on practically every issue, the United States voted to undercut the rights of the colonial people. This information is very important if one is to evaluate the current efforts of the U.S. to bring approximately six hundred islands in the Pacific under her exclusive control for an indefinite period of time.

New Africa had by the early fifties become so irritating to the colonial powers that the British government banned it in Kenya; but after continued pressure from Kenyans and a caustic letter from Alphaeus to the British Ambassador to the U.S. in Washington, the ban was reluctantly lifted.

Peekskill, N.Y.
Paul Robeson Concert
Aug. 27, 1949

Dashiell Hammett and Alphaeus on the way to jail, 1951

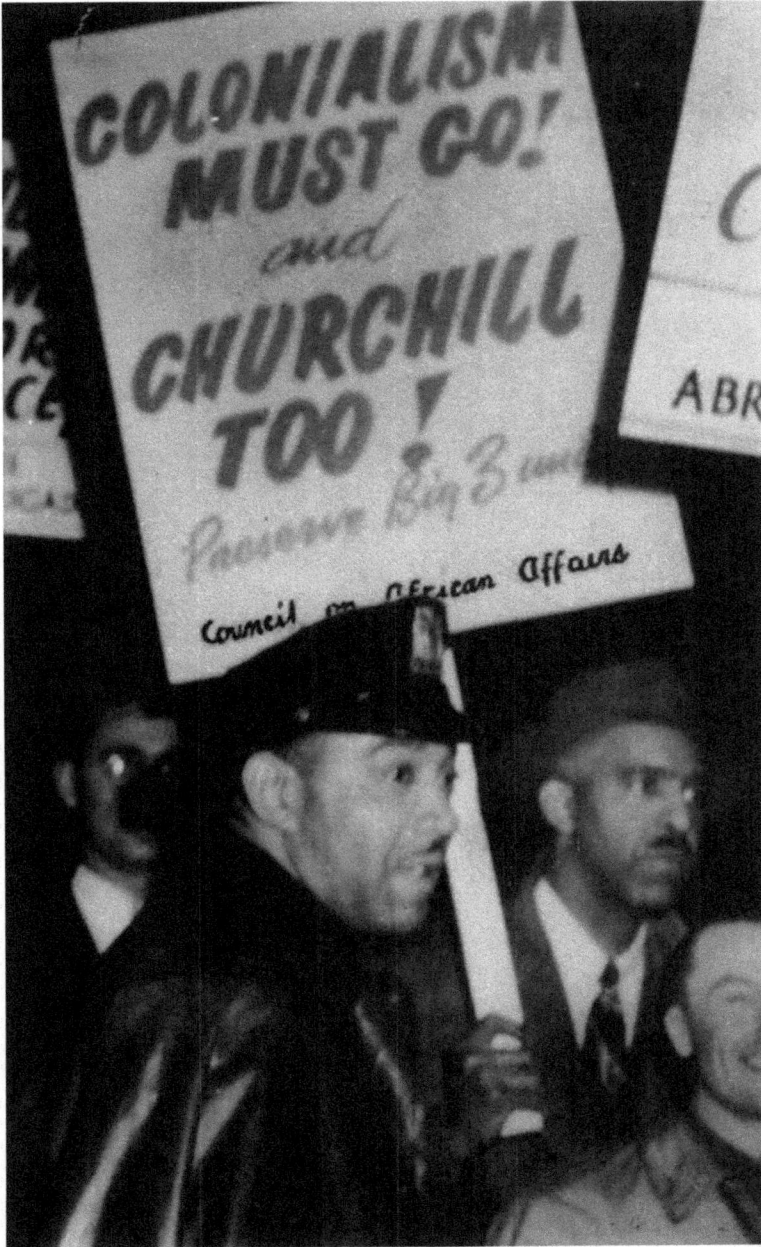

Picketing South African Consulate, April 1952

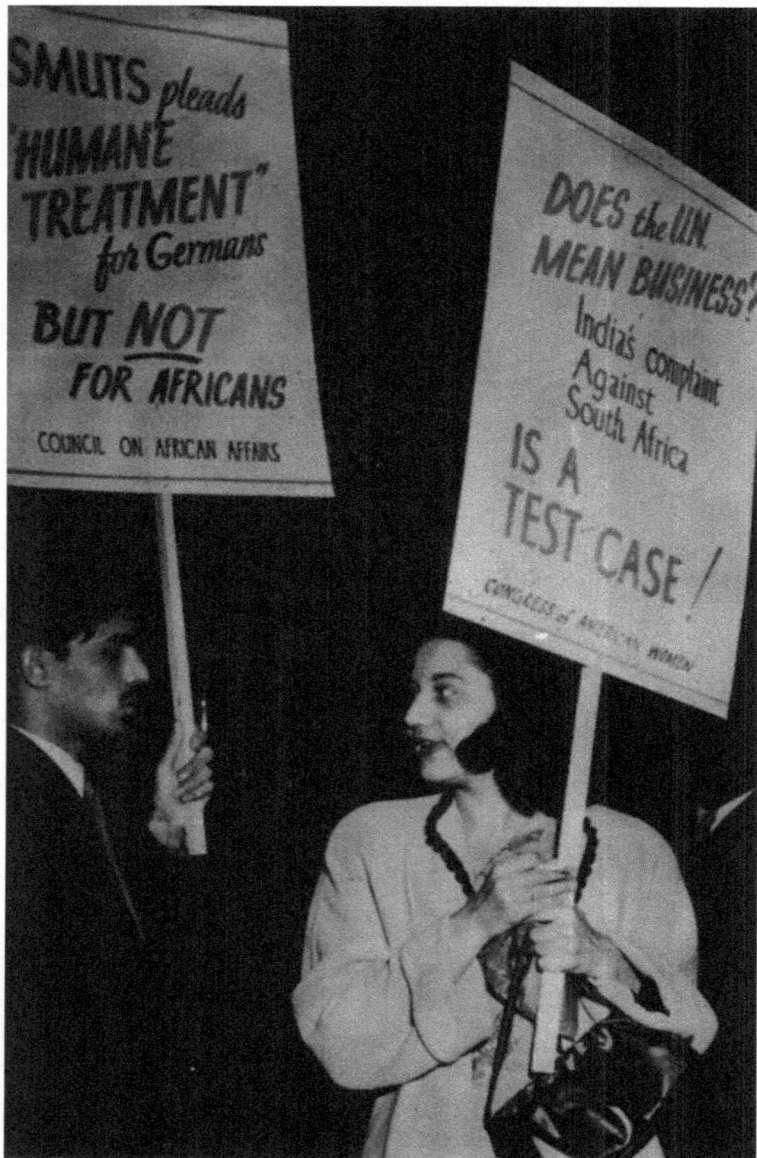

*E.S. Reddy (Former Director - Center Against Aparthied,
United Nations) and friend, 1946*

Josh Lawrence, Paul Robeson, Rev. Shelton Bishop and Adam C. Powell, Sr.,
are seated as Alphaeus Hunton, educational director of Council on
African Affairs, reads the resolutions to 4000 people at Abyssinia Baptist Church,
demanding freedom and liberties for the nations of South Africa.

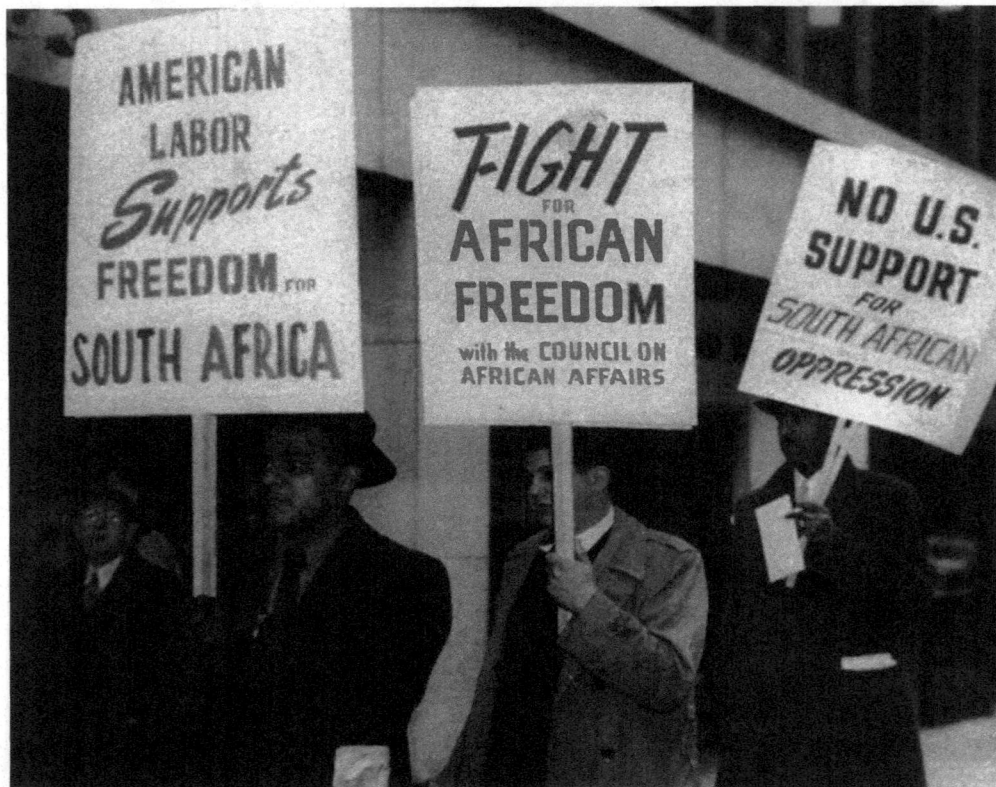

Picketing, 1952. South African Consulate
John Killens and Alphaeus

*Alphaeus' release from prison
with Dorothy, Paul Robeson and Dr. Du Bois*

---

6. THE COUNCIL ON AFRICAN AFFAIRS (PART II)

Long before the door of the Abyssinian Baptist Church in New York opened on January 7, 1946, the animated crowd milled around in small groups as they discussed the plight of the starving South African. Urgent pleas for help from the leaders of the stricken areas had prompted the Council to sponsor the mass meeting. A death-dealing famine gripped South Africa. For decades, since their reserves filled up and their soil eroded, Africans had suffered from hunger. Now, the food shortage afflicted them severely.

The church's 4,500 capacity quickly overflowed, and soon standing room no longer remained. Alphaeus hastily had loudspeakers connected in the basement, and the disappointed late comers assembled there. Judge Hubert Delany who chaired the rally characterized it as "one of the greatest ever held in Harlem."

Among the participants was Marian Anderson, the world famous contralto, who took time out from her heavy concert schedule to support the meeting. "What we do to help these people in Africa," Miss Anderson said, "will be a test of American democracy. Africans look to America with hope. We cannot fail them. Our aid to relieve the starvation in South Africa will be the measure of the degree to which Americans and particularly American Negroes, recognize that they themselves cannot find security as long as their brothers in other parts of the world live in hunger and want."

The enthusiastic gathering signalled the Council's long campaign in cooperation with Black and white businesses, churches, trade unions and community leaders to collect funds and canned goods for the relief of four million Africans facing starvation in the native reserves.

The keynote of the assembly, expressed repeatedly by all speakers, the audience voted to relay in a message to Dr. R. T. Bokwe who directed the distribution of supplies in one area. "We want our brothers and sisters to know," it said, "that the fight against discrimination in the United States can be won only as part of the war against human exploitation and oppression in South Africa and everywhere else. We are your allies, and together we shall achieve the final people's victory."

The audience demonstrated their eagerness to help by donating several thousand cans of food and $1,700. But it was just the beginning. After three months of intensive effort to arouse American support, Alphaeus called upon newspapers, churches and other institutions in forty cities to set aside March 31st as **Help Africa Day.**

While millions of Africans were living on a daily ration of three quarters of a pound of corn, when it was available, a diet far below the starvation line, the **New York Times** rated hungry baboons above the Africans as news. "Starving baboons plagued South Africa," blazed the May 25th headline. "Hunger resulting from prolonged drought in the South African belt has been driving troops of baboons from the mountains into cultivated areas...even into Cape Town itself."

That baboon story rated five inches of space, but neither the **New York Times** nor any other daily newspaper saw fit to publish one line regarding the extent of human starvation in the Union of South Africa.

In a letter to the **New York Times** editor, commenting on the news item, Alphaeus wrote: "Human beings, not merely animals are suffering starvation in South Africa. Isn't it about time we Americans started thinking about human beings, the Africans who inhabit the continent of Africa, rather than the wild animals and general flora and fauna, however 'exotic?'" The lack of information in the general press on famine conditions in South Africa was one of the important reasons for the Madison Square Garden meeting on June 6th, whereby the Council aimed to call attention of the American public to that and other problems affecting the people of Africa.

For weeks Alphaeus worked with groups organizing and publicizing the June rally with **"Big Three Unity for Colonial Freedom"** the theme, the second anniversary of the Allied invasion of Normandy, D-Day. Madison Square Garden, home of circuses and exciting athletic events, saw something quite different when more than 15,000 persons filled the huge arena, the largest audience ever assembled in the U.S. at a meeting on African freedom.

Brightly colored spotlights played upon the platform, where some of America's leading personalities and popular artists of stage and screen waited their turn to speak or perform. The list of participants seemed endless as the crowd roared, youths whistled, and cheers resounded when each speaker made his point. The meeting stressed United Nations unity to assure a speedy democratic solution to the colonial problem.

Few, if any, nations took into account the basic issue at large that the

British economist, Leonard Barnes, a council member, indicated in his message of greetings, that:

> the crucial point of the whole historical era in which we live is that democracy cannot come out on top, except with the active assistance of the dependent and exploited multitudes of tropical and sub-tropical lands. Our relationship with the multitudes is one of reciprocal needs. They cannot win their liberties without our help, and we cannot securely establish ours without theirs.

The fact that the South Africa government had placed a twenty-five percent duty charge on the 22,000 cans of food already shipped for distribution, thus compounding the grave situation, made the proceeds from the gathering more urgent. The rally climaxed six months of hard work for Alphaeus in the Council's nationwide drive, which netted substantial financial aid and 50,000 cans of food.

The last load of canned goods had hardly left New York when Alphaeus received news of another disaster in that oppressed land. It was August 12th, 1946, that the white ruling class of South Africa, accustomed to riding contentedly on the backs of its black workers, received a sudden and rude jolting. Two hundred thousand African miners employed in the gold fields of Johannesburg walked off their jobs in the largest strike the country had ever seen. It forced over a dozen mines to close, and created consternation among the operators and government authorities.

For six years, the miners, whose wages had remained at the level of £3 ($12.00) a month since 1900, had been petitioning for improvement of working conditions and increased salaries. They had received neither reply nor acknowledgment of any of their communications. Separated from their families for long periods of time, they lived cooped up in prison-like, walled in compounds, 20 to 80 in a room, and in some cases sleeping on bare concrete bunks. Vicious police dogs and barbed wire guarded the miners confined there for the duration of their contract, which ran from six to twelve months. Their food, given against their pay, often turned out to be inedible, causing them to resort to repeated hunger strikes. They worked ten to fourteen back-breaking hours; yet according to Prime Minister Smuts, they had no grievances.

The authorities, of course took reprisals at once. Truck loads of armed police, some carrying bayonets and rifles, rushed to the mines, immediately went into action, and quickly smashed the strike. "It is clearly apparent from the facts," Alphaeus wrote in the bulletin, "that the police action in crushing the strike represented the government working hand in glove with the wealthy mine owners and operators to keep the workers in continued servitude." Indeed they were. The police performed a brutal, thorough, mind breaking job for the Chamber of Mines, and in a period of six days, according to one source, at least thirty strikers were shot down or otherwise killed, not to mention the uncounted numbers beaten and seriously injured.

Despite the employers' spy system, general intimidation and exploitation of tribal differences among the workers, the miners displayed courage. They planned and executed their strike in the face of legal prohibitions against their exercising normal trade union rights, which showed their proletarian development. Desperation made them act. Defeat did not cow them nor was the strike the "work of agitators" as Smuts had the audacity to proclaim. It created more than an industrial battle. It opened a new chapter in the country's history and distinctly revealed the mine owner's dictatorship as the real government of the Union of South Africa.

Without delay, Alphaeus sent out press releases calling upon the American people to give "immediate expression of support for the 200,000 miners," declaring that, "the absentee and South African mine owners were seeking to preserve a form of industrial tyranny repugnant to every decent practice in modern employment." With the help of many organizations he arranged a conference where the participants agreed to give full support to an intensive campaign to bring the issue before the American public and secure favorable action by the United Nations.

A marked recession occurred in 1947 from the level of mass action developed in the preceding year. Actually, 1946 was the high point in the Council's influence; also the beginning of the Cold War. The Council initiated only one public affair directly in the interest of African freedom — its tenth anniversary celebration. There were at least four opportunities for action that it missed, however, due to the shortcomings of the Executive Director's office. The event dedicated to **African and Colonial Freedom Through a Strong United Nations**, took place at the 71st Regiment Armory in New York City, April 1947. A special dramatization, by John LaTouche, author of many shows, films and songs, highlighted the rally, which also marked Paul Robeson's birthday.

The play depicted the struggles of the African and colonial peoples to further their own welfare and promote their independence. "It was probably the most difficult thing I've ever written," confessed LaTouche. "There is no escaping the fact that this is 'One World' and colonial freedom is a must for world peace. And that involves us." He also disclosed that he had been warned by "well meaning people, I suppose," that it was extremely risky to his career to write that show. "The risk," he said, "I fear is to keep silent now." Many prominent people sent greetings, including Mrs. Eleanor Roosevelt, Albert Einstein, Leonard Bernstein, The Rev. Shelton Hale Bishop and Jawaharlal Nehru, to name a few.

The paramount questions raised in 1944, relative to strengthening the Council organizationally, had not been resolved; on the contrary, the situation had continued to deteriorate despite Alphaeus's efforts to build a strong foundation. The non-collective, one-man rule manner in which Yergan continued to function, with little or no discussion of the challenging issues at hand, left Alphaeus to work out projects at his own discretion to keep the work alive before the public.

At a time when the Council's efforts for the defense of the African people and their liberation should have been intensified, Yergan decided to withdraw from the militant struggle. More than once the action called for sharp criticism of United States policies which were clearly opposed to the welfare of the African people. Yet, Yergan actively fought against such proposals of action, seeking to conceal his own political retreat. During that period he repeatedly issued red-baiting statements to the press and directed irresponsible charges of "communism" against those Council members who insisted upon the defense of Africans against the increased exploitation and oppression under the so-called European Recovery Program ("Marshall Plan").

After sixteen years in Africa as a Y.M.C.A. secretary, where Yergan smoldered under the coals of imperialism while carrying out his activities there, he became dissatisfied with the slow pace of the organization, which certainly had no thought of changing its program. Yergan wanted to hit hard at colonial rule, but to do so under the structure of the Y.M.C.A. set up was not possible. He needed an organization tied to no foundation and independent of all political parties. Its one objective would be to aid downtrodden Africans. With that in mind, he helped to form the Council on African Affairs. Now, he made peace with the House Un-American Activities Committee, the U.S. Justice Department and the thousand and one official and unofficial "loyalty boards." The associations which twelve years before he had blasted so vehemently he renewed, and he set as his goal the disruption of the Council's work and discrediting the organization before the public. A bitter struggle over policy and control ensued and the majority membership ousted Yergan. As a result Alphaeus became the Executive Secretary, Paul Robeson remained Chairman, Dr. W.E.B. Du Bois, Vice-Chairman, and Estelle Osborne, Treasurer.

Normal conditions gradually prevailed after months of frustrations and counter activities. Alphaeus gave top priority on the new agenda to building the slowly waning membership. With Paul Robeson, the Director of Organization, Louise Thompson Patterson, made a cross-country tour in the hope of netting a few local chapters. Louise Patterson, wife of the noted Civil Rights lawyer, William L. Patterson, who dropped a successful law practice to devote his energies to the defense of civil rights, had extensive organizational experience and came well equipped to head the Council's intensive membership drive, which was long overdue. Unfortunately, the political atmosphere at that time hampered the possibility of a successful campaign.

The first sign of the Cold War came quickly after President Harry S. Truman sided with Winston Churchill's provocative "Iron Curtain" speech in Fulton, Missouri, in 1946. Churchill hinted that atomic war might threaten the world. Truman had already shown his heartlessness by dropping two atomic bombs on the Japanese people without military justification and killing a quarter of a million and maiming countless others. He chose a horrid method with which to warn the U.S.S.R. of American power and bring the war to a speedy end.

Conditions shifted to a drastic level when Truman took his cue from preceding events and issued his infamous executive order in March 1947, establishing a loyalty program for the Federal government that strengthened the already powerful House Un-American Activities Committee (H.U.A.C.). It also set a pattern for private employers and public agencies to take like action based on the Attorney General's list. The government became so obsessed with the idea of communism, which they were desperately trying to halt in Korea, and later in Vietnam, without success, that they lost sight completely of the real danger to world peace, the oppression of the darker races. Alphaeus more than once spoke of the uselessness of trying to keep the world safe for democracy anywhere until the people everywhere got on equal terms with one another in every respect. On the other hand, he knew there could be no overtures to equal terms until colonial dependence ceased.

Repeated attacks on individuals and organizations made Alphaeus's work extremely difficult. Nevertheless, he continued to rally aid and support on many issues in time of crisis in African affairs. There were the Gold Coast strike in 1948, with the arrest of Kwame Nkrumah and other leaders; the coal miners' strike in Enugu, Nigeria, in 1949 (for a basic pay of eighty cents a day), which ended with the brutal slaying of twenty-six workers; the U.N. decision in 1949, on the status of Italy's former African colonies; the French government's wholesale arrest, killings, and campaign of terror against the Rassemblement Democratic African in French West Africa the same year, and the shooting down of African workers on American-owned rubber and iron ore properties in Liberia in 1950.

The single African event that attracted the greatest public attention in 1950, was the British government's order exiling Seretse Khama, leader of the Bamansgwato people, from his homeland, which is now Botswana. Seretse Khama's marriage to a white woman brought the wrath of the colonial government down of his head. **New Africa,** the first publication in this country to bring the central issue to the notice of the public, analyzed and ventilated the motive. The act symbolized the racial chauvinism and tyrannical dictatorship which in general characterized the relations of the

British, French, Belgians and other foreign overloads with their African sublects.

For nearly a year Alphaeus kept the burning subject alive in the bulletin, and secured endorsement of a petition to the United Nations demanding justice for Seretse Khama and the Bamanagwato people. Seretse Khama, who became President of the Republic of Botswana, deeply appreciated the Council's support. "It is pleasant and reassuring to know that Africans overseas and those of African descent remain conscious of our homeland and its welfare," he wrote. "My wife and I will always be indebted to you."

7. PRISON: THE BAIL FUND AFFAIR

Along with the intensified practice of establishing guilt by unsupported accusations, and character assassination by alleged association, there grew steadily a pattern of linking the advocacy of full equality for Blacks and minorities with Un-Americanism. Frequently, in examinations designed to test the loyalty of applicants for government positions, the question was asked whether they believed in equality of the white and black races or entertained Blacks in their homes. It was not unusual in many areas for those defending non-segregated housing to be branded as Communists. Long ago those who pleaded for low cost housing had been called Socialist.

Bitter experience has taught us that the emotional attitude of a people can be nurtured and shaped by a cruel and clever government to any end the rulers may wish. McCarthyism spewed the menacing influence in the fifties. Drunk with power, the junior senator from Wisconsin, Joseph R. McCarthy, commanded national attention in his reckless crusade to eliminate so-called Communism from every aspect of American life. He constantly fed the public the big lie of our time, with his rabid, obsessive idea of security risks in the Federal Government.

In the early forties, the horrors of the Dies Committee investigations had set the precedent for the new McCarthy inquisitions. McCarthy's authority reached even into the U.S. overseas libraries, where hundreds of books by forty authors were yanked from the shelves by the State Department. Oddly, outstanding among the works singled out for elimination were the distinguished contributions on the subject of race discrimination, especially anti-Black oppression in the U.S. The purpose was, of course, to sow the seeds of suspicion of those writers who had the nerve to reveal or reject American racial inequalities. Weren't they adhering to the Red line? Consequently, their writings must be subversive.

In such an inhibitive atmosphere of red-baiting and war hysteria, Alphaeus organized a picket line of more than a hundred in front of

Madison Square Garden to protest the refusal of the Garden to permit the Council to hold a concert-rally, featuring Paul Robeson. The event held in September of 1950 had two purposes; to protest the revocation of Robeson's passport, and to demonstrate public support for Dr. W. E. B. Du Bois, who faced a five-year jail term if convicted for his refusal to register under the Foreign Agents Registration Act, as chairman of the Peace Information Center.

After the demonstration, Alphaeus said:

> It is no accident that a progressive Negro organiza-
> tion, the Council on African Affairs, and a great
> Negro leader like Paul Robeson, have been made the
> first target of the proposed police state legislation.
> The fight to compel the Garden Corporation to
> reverse its stand is joined with the struggle to defeat
> the Wood-Mundt-McCarran-Kilgore repressive bills.

Among the untold number of organizations on the H.U.A.C.'s subversive list was the Council on African Affairs and the Civil Rights Congress. The **C.R.C.**, of which William L. Patterson was National Executive Secretary, derived from a merger of the International Labor Defense and the National Federation of Constitutional Liberties. It was formed in 1946 to conduct struggles for the legal defense of victims of American reaction. When private bonding companies refused to provide bail for progressives, but had no hesitation in granting it to gangsters, thieves and the like, it became necessary to provide some kind of fund, and a group of public minded citizens set up the **Civil Rights Bail Fund.**

Contributions came in from thousands of people from every political persuasion and every sphere of life. Four trustees were secured to administer the fund: Dashiell Hammett, the noted mystery novelist, who had been a part of the struggle for more than a decade; Frederick Vanderbilt Field, editor and writer on the Far East, and a member of the prestigious Vanderbilt family; Abner Green, Executive Secretary of the **Committee for the Protection of the Foreign Born,** a man whom thousands of foreign born remembered with affection and gratitude, and Alphaeus.

Those four men held their sacrifices as unimportant in a just cause. For refusing to hand over the records to the committee, they were sentenced to six months in prison for contempt of court. Frederick Field, in violation of the Fifth Amendment, was subjected to double peril and sentenced twice; once for six months and once for three months for the same crime

That fateful morning, July 9, 1951, when the gathering clouds of obstruction threw a shadow of gloom over our lives, is etched indelibly in my memory. Just two weeks previous we had moved into our own home, on a quiet block in Queens, New York. It was the only house owned by Blacks for years in that area. Its last owner was a close family friend who had recently died. Having vistited her for many summers, I knew the neighbors in the adjoining homes — one German, the other Irish, and these acquaintances proved very valuable in the trying months ahead.

As Alphaeus and I sat at the breakfast table discussing the coming events of the day (he was to appear in court at 11:30 to answer charges against the Civil Rights Bail Fund), he casually commented on the fact that Field had been sentenced the day before and he expected the same fate. The impact of what he said did not really penetrate at the moment. The situation had never been seriously discussed prior to that morning. Alphaeus viewed the predicament in such a nonchalant manner that one would have thought he was merely going to the office as usual.

What if they locked him up immediately? We had made no plans to cover any problems that would arise. There had been no time to sit down and discuss seriously the numerous things that had to be done. The roof leaked; the furnace had to be replaced, and alterations made. How could I cope with all the new problems in that old house?

A million questions ran through my mind as we hurried to reach court on time. Like most wives, who more often than not are taken for granted and inadequately consulted on important issues that concern them as well as their husbands, I was left with the assumption that, somehow I would manage. Whatever the reason, I was totally unprepared to see Alphaeus put behind bars that morning.

A sense of numbness crept over me as I watched the courtroom procedure. Alphaeus had continued to answer the judge in his soft, quiet voice, refusing to disclose the names of the contributors. Now it was finished! The guard came forward, took him away, locked him up. Court was dismissed until afternoon when he would be sentenced. Dazed and bewildered, I walked out into the street, wondering what to do next. The need to talk to someone became more and more urgent as I racked my brain, searching for the right person. One had to be careful in that out-of-focused period when innocent people were often exposed to public scorn by mere association. Nevertheless, my friend Nellie Stanly, whose secretarial job in the school system could have been in danger by her friendship with us, put aside her family tasks and accompanied me to court.

"Six months for contempt of court," continued to ring in my ears as I prepared for bed that night, alone in our house amid unpacked barrels, boxes, and disarranged furniture. Never had I felt so devastated, crushed and utterly deserted. For the first time in my life I had to stand alone.

Yet from the agony and bitter experience of that day, a new insight into myself and the nature of emotional pressure emerged. That new and enlightening awareness dispelled any doubts I may have had about my ability to meet boldly any future calamities.

Those were frightening years, years that tried men's souls and spread distrust through the silence of fear that gripped the hearts and minds of progressive America. My German neighbor, an elderly, aggressive woman, who spent much of her time sitting on the bench in her front yard, was a plucky match for the inquisitive, the curious, and the F.B.I. who parked across the street in front of our house every day for weeks. Though I never saw them (they came after I left for work and pulled out before I returned), she kept me well informed; not only of them, but of the interviews by the press with certain neighbors.

The whole rotten affair distressed and depressed me, but it did not compare to the harassment and terrifying experiences heaped upon courageous Esther Jackson and her two small children during that period. Esther, now the managing editor of **Freedomways**, is the wife of Dr. James Jackson, who was then a leader in the communist party in the southern states. Jackson had been indicted under the Smith Act, but had become a political refugee. The F.B.I. was so vexed because he had slipped through their fingers that their agents inflicted systematic revenge on his family, down to their four-year-old daughter, who had a constant F.B.I. escort each day on her way to nursery school.

The Smith Act, a thought control law, placed new and unconstitutional restrictions on the right to freedom of speech and political association. It aimed to punish people for their ideas, and the right to advocate ideas distasteful to the rulers of our government; for acting together to achieve common objectives — such as uniting in the struggle against the threat of war, unbridled oppression, and economic hardships. The first victims to be tried and convicted were the top Communist leaders, among whom were two Blacks. Benjamin Davis, whose father served as a G.O.P. national committeeman in Georgia, was raised in luxury, Amherst-educated, and had a law degree from Harvard. Yet he turned his back on what could have been a life of leisure, to fight for a dangerous, and to him a just cause. The Harlem community elected him twice to serve on the New York City Council. He fought on many fronts with Henry Winston. Winston, who is still a stalwart Communist leader with a long, courageous record of struggle for American youth, the rights of Blacks and the working class, was sentenced to eight years under a Smith Act frameup, and became totally blind as a result of deliberate neglect of his health in prison. Only after world-wide protest was he released after serving five years.

Recalling the Black man's direct experience through generations of historical struggles against "informers," and one that continues to have special significance for our efforts to achieve equality as citizens in all areas of American life, one is reminded of similar instances. Time and again, leaders of color have been confronted by official and unofficial despots with the demand: "Tell us the name of your associates!" Time and again those leaders refused to act as informers for the oppressors of their people, even at the risk of their personal liberty or lives. They refused to degrade themselves on the high moral ground that the cause for which they and their colleagues labored was just and to name their associates would be to betray them to the wrath of immoral, illegal, and prejudice-ridden forces of persecution.

"Who can remember the name of the craven slave who betrayed Denmark Vesey?" read the editorial of **Freedom**, Paul Robeson's paper, on which Alphaeus served as an Editorial Board member. "Or the miserable fellow who told his master the details of the plan when Nat Turner struck for freedom at Southhampton? Their names are buried with their bones in ignominious graves.

"Harriet Tubman and Sojourner Truth are the shining exemplars of our struggling womanhood; Douglass remains the paragon of unyielding leadership; John Brown is sainted in our midst; Vesey, Turner and Prosser clothed with life the words of a song which guided a whole people: 'Before I'd be a slave I'll be buried in my grave and go home to my Lord and be free.'

"These men and women were trustees of our bloody struggles for freedom. They were worthy of their trust and history shows they merited the responsibility they cherished for their lives and liberation of millions of oppressed bondsmen. They would and did, protect their trust with their lives.

"Add to theirs the name of Hunton."

"I am sure you share my deep concern over the imprisonment of Dr. William A. Hunton for the refusal to betray his trust as an officer of the Civil Rights Bail Fund," wrote Dr. W.E.B. Du Bois, to a number of prominent Black citizens, August 8, 1951, for the **Special Committee on Dr. W. A. Hunton.** "I have come to know this fine man very well during my years of association with the Council on African Affairs. Quiet, studious, conscientious and absolutely uncorruptible, he is the worthy son of a fine and distinguished family from which he comes.

"A vindictive prosecutor and court have sent Dr. Hunton to jail for six months for so-called contempt of court. He does not belong there, and I hope you will join me in trying to get him out."

Dr. Du Bois' proposal was to ask several hundred Black leaders to endorse a petition to the President and Attorney General, urging an immediate pardon for Alphaeus. In that distressing episode in our history, it took courage and grit to sign a petition for one in Alphaeus's position. The

Administration frequently ignored the petition and at times victimized the petitioners. Nevertheless, fifty-four Black leaders from twenty-two states affixed their names. Yet, the petition brought no response from the government. Alphaeus was denied bail, pending an appeal and he eked out his time at the Jim-Crow Federal Prison in Petersburg, Virginia, working in the small, poorly stocked library.

In September **An Open Letter to J. Howard McGrath**, U.S. Attorney General, concerning the four trustees appeared in magazines and newspapers across the country under the sponsorship of Elmer Benson, former Governor of Minnesota; Fred Stover, President of the Iowa Farmers Union; Robert W. Kenny, former Attorney General of California; William Hood, Secretary of Local 600, United Automobile Workers; I.F. Stone, journalist, and Professor Robert Morss Lovett. Thousands of Americans from every state in the Union and from all levels of life gave their signatures and their dollars to bring the message to their fellow citizens. But it was of no avail.

McCarthy, the most infamous of the self-righteous chauvinists to undertake the ruination of innocent people's careers, aroused public anxieties about Communism to fanatical proportions. The reactions he provoked, the crudeness of his political style, and his debating tactics kept him in the news. Yet McCarthy did not work in isolation. The House Un-American Activities Committee, of which Richard Nixon was an energetic and inflexible member, existed long before and after. Public pressure, however, finally cut the senator down to size in 1955, after five years of blind untruths that deluded great numbers of people, and left behind untold damage to countless others, victims of a shattered society.

In the months following Alphaeus's imprisonment, I floundered through a rising tide of conflicting emotions. To be objective did not come easily. The indifference and unfeeling attitude of some people with whom I had been associated for twenty-five years, perplexed me. I suppose economics becomes closely connected to moral courage when one has passed the fanciful idealism of youth. Yet it seemed to make one's feelings known. The lack of concern for one's fellow member going through a shattering experience, when a kind, understanding word meant more than anything else, cut sharply and brought to light the true value of friendship. All this ushered in a deeper awareness of my place beside Alphaeus, and of our bond with all progressives working to make this a better world.

On my first trip to Petersburg, it was not a pretty sight to behold Alphaeus's tall, gaunt figure in his misfitting prison garb. His six feet four and a half inches posed a problem for the clothing manager, but they were not about to make any new uniforms for him. He had lost several pounds, which he could ill-afford, and his face looked haggard and drawn. Yet he complained only about the food. Surely the bed was too short, and his feet extended far beyond the end; they always did in a normal size, like many human devices that were a fraction too small or skimpy for his need.

Meetings and more meetings consumed my evenings while Alphaeus was away, especially those of Black women who came together to discuss and do something about the many grievances they carried in their hearts. The time had come to personally address the government for immediate and unconditional redress of injustices suffered at the hands of organized bigotry. To that end a committee sent **A Call to Negro Women** throughout the land to come to Washington, D.C., September 29 through October 1st, 1951, to demand an audience with the President, the Justice Department, and the State Department.

The Sojourners for Truth and Justice, as we were called, one hundred and thirty-two Black women from various sections of the country, and all walks of life, assembled in Washington at the home of Frederick Douglass; heard their proclamation read..."In the spirit of Sojourner Truth and Harriet Tubman," it declared, "we shall not be trampled upon any longer."

They were there to unite and dedicate themselves to fight unceasingly for the rights of our people, and for full dignity of Black womanhood. For three days the Sojourners held forth. A special appointment was made with Maceo Hubbard in the Civil Rights Section of the Justice Department. Mr. Hubbard, a Black, appeared painfully disturbed as sixty Black women entered his office while a single white government official stood with folded arms, surveying the group. A number of women had their say, and when they had finished, we felt a bit sorry for Mr. Hubbard, sitting behind the big desk, making it easier for some white official who was guilty of the crimes we related.

"Be sure to get Alphaeus on that plane," was the last remark I heard as I left New York to bring him home. A large delegation would be at the airport to greet him the following day, and to miss the scheduled flight would have been unthinkable. With one month off for good behavior, Alphaeus was released on December 9th.

The excitement of preparing for the trip, two sleepless nights, and the mixup and confusion among the friends who were to take us to the airport had left me in a frightful dither. I wanted to look my best and feel even better, but I felt and looked my worst. When the plane took off, I too took off, right in the paper bag before me for some relief. Little did my friend realize how sick I was, when she said, "For God's sake, Dorothy, smile," and presented me with a beautiful bouquet of red roses. I did try. It was Alphaeus's day, and I rejoiced in his return, but I thought any minute I would buckle under.

More than a hundred black and white friends greeted Alphaeus as he stepped off the plane at LaGuardia Airport in a misty rain. "Welcome home, Dr. Hunton," they cried. Some carried placards acclaiming him a "Defender of the Bill of Rights." The present thrust in his hand by his friend and co-worker Dr. Herbert Aptheker delighted him. It was a copy of the **Documentary History of the Negro People** he had compiled, and which the Federal Prison Authorities in Petersburg refused to let him receive when it came in the mail.

"I wanted this book — with its priceless speeches and writings by Frederick Douglass and other great spokesmen of freedom, very,very, badly," Alphaeus said. "But the wardens thought it was too inflammatory, and feared it would cause a race riot if many of the prisoners read it. Many of the prisoners were sharecroppers and workers. They were very friendly and sympathetic and promised to help in the struggle for their people when they got out."

In late December, the Sojourners organized a reception for Alphaeus and me at Small's Paradise in Harlem. It was an evening of rejoicing; a moving event that I recall to mind with warmth and pleasure.

Disregarding my entreaties to stay home a few days to get himself together, Alphaeus wasted no time in returning to the office. A stickler for duty and the sanctity of obligations, he knew that many critical issues had developed in Africa during his absence, and he was eager to resume his work, always the pivot of his life.

"I'm glad to be back with you," he wrote in the first issue of **Spotlight on Africa** after his return. "It has been indeed heart-warming to receive the greetings and good wishes of many Council members and friends since my return to New York from my enforced 'vacation'...I want to take this means of saying, Hello to all you near and far, including especially my friends and colleagues in many sections of Africa.

"I come back to what prison inmates call the 'free world'--a world in which things are getting more and more difficult for the imperialist overlords. As we in the Council have long forseen, the explosive national resistance to foreign domination has spread from Asia to Africa. What does this mean to us in the United States? Plenty!"

The brutal armed suppression of the National Liberation Movements in Tunisia and Morocco was in full swing when Alphaeus returned. After two hours of picketing in support of the demand for Tunisian freedom and Security Council action to prevent an outbreak of war in North Africa, Alphaeus led a large delegation to the French Consul. In the meantime, South Africa's ten million non-whites continued their struggle through the heroic **Campaign of Defiance of Unjust Laws** during 1952.

In response to an urgent appeal from South Africa for aid of the children and families of more than 8,000 men and women who were sent to jail, during the campaign the Council collected and forwarded $2,500. Alphaeus also organized a picket line in front of the South African Consulate and the South African Delegation to the U.N. It was in connection with that campaign that he wrote the pamphlet,**Resistance with a Postcript for Americans.**

Scarcely a day passed when he did not grapple with some problem somewhere in Africa. South Africa had always been in the forefront, with the situation growing more acute daily. Now, Kenya. The basic cause of the conflict there was precisely the same. In February, 1944, Alphaeus wrote an article in the bulletin **What about Kenya?** in which he described the East African colony, twice the size of Great Britain and Ireland, as "one of the most extreme of Africa's sore spots." A vital part of Britain's extensive African empire, they constantly cracked down on any African organization united for self-rule. **The Kenya African Union** was the latest target; founded in 1944, it became the greatest movement for the Africans. Now, on October 21, 1952, its President, Jomo Kenyatta, and other leaders, had been arrested and a state of emergency declared.

Britain's "dirty war" in Kenya was a long and brutal one. They used the suppression of the violent insurrection "Mau Mau," as an excuse of the most horrendous, genocidal crimes against the Kikuyu people. Alphaeus planned an all-day working conference (April 24, 1954) in Harlem, which resulted in a program of assistance, and setting up the **National Aid Committee.** Street corner meetings were held in order to give the busy Harlemite a vivid picture of events happening to his brothers and sisters in Kenya. He must be made to see the connection between colonialism and Jim Crow, and the common objectives for which Kenya Africans and Blacks in Mississippi and Harlem struggled.

For more than two hours speaker after speaker took the microphone and spoke their minds. The response was good. Passersby stayed to listen, bought "Africa Must be Free" buttons, copies of the bulletin, and anything else concerning Africa. The meetings demonstrated the people's ready support for the Council's program to **Aid to Kenya Africans** if only they could get the truth, and know **how** to help.

With all the monumental problems confronting Alphaeus in running the organization, an additional one was added in June 1955. After months of harassment and investigations, the Council began its legal fight to continue functioning. The Federal Grand Jury in Washington subpoenaed Alphaeus to appear October 7, 1955. He had to present all correspondence with the African National Congress, and the South African Indian Congress, which jointly led the struggle in South Africa. As if that were not enough, they demanded all other correspondence from 1946 to 1955, all records of funds sent abroad, and all materials published or disseminated by the Council during the same nine year poriod.

The jury quizzed Alphaeus at length regarding funds and food sent to relieve the South African famine in 1946-7, and funds sent to aid the dependents of those jailed during the **Campaign of Defense of Unjust**

Laws. The Grand Jury said it was concerned with whether the activities represented violation of the Foreign Registration Act.

Alphaeus replied that the Council of African Affairs had never been the agent of any foreign principal, and consequently had never considered the question of registration as such. The real issue in the case, he said, was the moral question of whether it was right or wrong for Americans to give assistance to Africans suffering and in dire need. The Justice Department counsel gave a clue to the underlying purpose of the proceedings, when he asked why Negroes in America should feel that they have any common cause with the people of Africa, and why the Council maintained that the U.S. Government should give no further loans or other aid to the South African Government. Those questions Alphaeus answered in no uncertain terms.

For three years after his release from prison, Alphaeus fought a losing battle with the government in defense of the right to advocate and support the cause of African freedom. Never endowed with a working fund, the non-partisan, non-profit Council on African Affairs (C.A.A.) ran solely on contributions, and was staffed mostly with volunteer help. Few volunteers were available for the many pressing office tasks, and Alphaeus found himself practically a one-man organization, persevering under the most trying conditions and working late into the night without pay. Though he never confided his anguish to me, I knew his heart was overcast with despair, while he tried unsuccessfully to disguise his inner feelings. It was infinitely more painful for me to watch him literally drag himself to the office day after day, being stripped of vitality and enthusiasm for life, than to experience it myself.

Yet, as I watched his shoulders droop more and more, and his steps began to falter, my anxiety for him mounted. Finally, I could stand it no longer. "African freedom or no African freedom," I screamed, "it's senseless to kill yourself from overwork, no matter how important the cause." As we sat on the divan trying to sort out our thoughts and emotions, after my sudden outburst, the silence deepened. Alphaeus lifted his tired, drained face, and his dark brown eyes, filled with sorrow, sought mine for a fleeting moment, as if in search for an answer to my unexpected flareup. Slowly he drew me close and gently kissed my tears away, and in his quiet soft voice, calmly but firmly promised to stop.

At the Executive Board meeting June 14, 1955, to decide whether the Council should continue, Alphaeus reviewed the organization's work during his twelve years of activity. He stressed the importance of the pioneering character of the work. It had been the only organization of its type in the United States giving full attention to the African people's problems and struggles.

He then traced the reason for the rapid growth of American interest in

Africa since 1952, which was reflected in popular and scholarly journals and books, in academic and governmental circles, and in the emergence of new organizations with aims and programs of work similar to those of the Council. He spoke of the heightened concern with African and colonial problems on the part of Black organizations with other main interests.

"In view of the changed situation and the possibility of American support for the African people's freedom being expressed through a wide range of other existing groups," Alphaeus noted, "the Council is no longer needed to stimulate American interest in Africa as in the earlier period of its work and it should accordingly be dissolved."

He stated also that "continuing government harassment of the organization had made it difficult if not impossible for it to function." He cited the various investigations to which the Council's finances and affairs had been subjected, and the intolerable strain which would be placed upon it by the hearing before the Subversive Activities Control Board, scheduled to start July 11.

Even so, Alphaeus said he would "recommend continuing to fight for the right to function, were it not for the considerations previously cited." Looking at the problem as a whole, he was convinced that dissolution of the Council was the only sensible course.

Thus Alphaeus ended twelve years of service to the organization and to the cause of African liberation in the face of great difficulties and personal sacrifice. He had tenaciously kept the faith, and had become a victim, along with countless others, of five years of demagogic hysteria, which found its outlet in hate, mistrust, and intolerance that in turn poisoned every facet of American life.

The closing down of the Council did not mean, however, that Alphaeus was giving up the fight, despite the pressures and blows from those who feared his voice as well as his existence. As Paul Robeson said, "Having done all, stand!" That Alphaeus did. It was a sad commentary on our times that one of the few organizations devoted to fighting the evils of colonialism had been red-baited into silence by a gestapo committee, which claimed a monopoly on what they termed "Americanism."

Letters poured in from wellwishers at home and abroad, expressing sadness regarding the dissolution of the Council. Alphaeus was gratified by the warm response. He had done all that was humanly possible to give the movement for African freedom momentum, and his unselfish and effective devotion to a momentous cause would not be forgotten.

In this desolate period of Alphaeus' life, dramatic developments were taking place in Asia and particularly Africa, which was no longer the "Dark Continent" but instead aglow, and in some places afire. He had been unable to attend the historic Asian-African Conference at Bandung, Indonesia, in April 1955, because of the critical situation surrounding the

Council and its imminent closing. However, the powerful impact of the representatives of more than two-thirds of the world's population struggling against colonialism and racialism and in the interest of peace, prompted him to dedicate the last two issues of the bulletin April-May, 1955 to the conference.

A survey of the African press gave the impression that the subject was less publicized and discussed there than in the United States. It was not because of the Africans' apathy. The curtain of censorship and repression with which the rulers of Africa sought to keep its people isolated from the mainstream of world affairs — except when needed to fight European wars — was responsible.

To the African and Asian, the opposition to color discrimination is so deeply felt that nations, otherwise at odds, unite regardless of divisive ideologies, particularly when they have shared misery and humiliation. They met to impress on the world that it is possible to live together, meet together, speak to each other, without losing one's identity, and yet contribute to the understanding of matters of common concern. It was possible to develop a true consciousness of the interdependence of men and nations for their well-being and survival of the earth.

Bandung was a shining light and a landmark in the annals of civilization. It reflected the determination of the Asian and African people to be done with Western dictation, and their determination to think for themselves and decide their own destiny. That Third World alignment struck fear in the minds of the white imperialist nations, and it continues to have repercussions today.

8. BROADENING HORIZONS

Free from the vexations and plaguing problems of a persecuted organization, Alphaeus devoted all of his time to research and writing **Decision in Africa,** which was published in 1957. In March of the same year, Vice-President Nixon made a rather jubilant tour of eight African countries. According to the **New Age,** a Johannesburg newspaper, "he worked hard to save Africa from communism," perhaps to keep it safe as a source for American profits. Nixon did a great deal of talking about his sympathy for the African's national aspiration.

The truth was that Africa's most hated government then and now, South Africa's Nationalists, teetering on the brink of economic and political disaster in the late forties and early fifties, had been literally saved by the direct assistance received from the U.S. when other countries were frightened away by their apartheid policies. Thus, the U.S. was instrumental in keeping the Nationalists in power and reinforcing racial oppression, which is the foundation of the country's great wealth in gold and diamonds.

It is to America that the government now looks for the bulk of foreign investment capital, and the list of American corporations doing business there is long. Since they are known for their hard bargaining acumen, their industries are well entrenched.

How the United States came to apartheid's rescue is vividly told in **Decision in Africa,** a carefully documented story of the unbridled and wasteful plunder of a continent solely for the benefit of the western world, with little regard for the welfare of the people whose natural resources were looted. The book is frequently used as a textbook and reference source, and has been translated into seven languages, including Chinese.

"I know of no one today," Dr. W.E.B. Du Bois wrote in the Foreward, "who has a more thorough knowledge and understanding of that continent than Dr. Hunton." He went on to say:

Today, after colonial imperialism has flourished two centuries in Asia and Africa, the recoil of the people of these continents against European aggression is the beginning of a new world development. However, our American attitude towards Black people is leading us to neglect and forget the great uprisings of the African peoples. This book, then, with its broad sweep and deep knowledge of what is happening in Africa and the development of present conditions from recent past, is invaluable. In a day when facts about Africa are habitually distorted or even concealed, this book presents a wealth of figures available nowhere else and invaluable not only for understanding Africa but for understanding Europe and America, which are becoming increasingly dependent on Africa for their future development.

A cruel fact of life confronted Alphaeus after compilation of his book; his academic opportunities narrowed down to the vanishing point. Like other departments of government, there was little democratic functioning of our schools and colleges at that point in history. Teachers and professors were in effect being forced into becoming informers under coercion and threat of economic ruin, without ever being permitted to confront their accusers, or even to know their identity.

All doors to the academic world were blocked to Alphaeus, and he was actually reduced to the level of taking anything he could get to keep his self-respect and sanity. Eventually, he found employment in the Hudson Bay Fur Company in 1957, and worked as a seasonal employee in the IBM department for four consecutive seasons until April 1960. Strange, none of his co-workers called him Alphaeus. Everyone knew him as "Bill," the familiar nickname his father loved; perhaps he did also.

One aspect of the African's dream of repossessing his continent and becoming master of his country's destiny slowly unfolded when the former British Colony, the Gold Coast vanished from the map March 6, 1957, and the ancient name of the Kingdom Ghana, distinguished the new, independent nation. Having made substantial sacrifices in two world wars, only to be cheated out of their promised freedom, the African people accelerated the tempo of nationalism, particularly in West Africa, and a new surge for Africanization arose.

Dr. Kwame Nkrumah, a young firebrand, American and British educated, a former school teacher and a shrewd politician, fought hard for Ghana's independence. Around the bend, on the western "Hump" of Africa, Guinea, fed up with French domination said no to General

DeGaulle when he offered all 13 French colonies in Africa their choice of semi-independence in a "French Community" or going it alone as an independent state without subsidies. Led by Sekou Touré, a militant young leftist and Pan Africanist, the founder and leader of the powerful Union General des Travailleurs de L'Afrique Noire, the country voted for a full break. It was the only colony that did, and Guinea became a Republic, September 28, 1958, the ninth independent African ruled state. Now, tense excitement grew as the Ghanaians completed plans for the All African People's Conference, held in Accra, December 8, 1959.

While visiting William and Louise Patterson, we discussed excitedly the African conference. John Gray, a friend of long standing, said very forcefully, "Alphaeus should attend the conference by all means." Everyone agreed, of course. How would he get there? He had neither the money nor a passport, and it was just one week before the opening. Impossible! Heads promptly got together, however, and it was decided that he must go. Immediately they formulated plans to raise money. A list was prepared of friends to see — this string to pull and that call to make. In one hour the group organized to see that Alphaeus reached Accra in time for that historic event.

Early next morning he left for Washington to secure his passport. Without a hitch it was granted, and within four days, the money received surpassed, by far, their expectations. The circumstances moved so smoothly and swiftly that Alphaeus could scarcely believe his good fortune.

"The historic **All African People's Conference** represented the convergence of the maturing, liberating forces of the continent," Alphaeus wrote in the postscript of the revised edition of **Decision in Africa, 1960.** He added:

> The main emphasis on that assembly was unity. Dr. Nkrumah noted that the Conference had helped us to discover the source of our weakness, that is, the division within our ranks. Now we are resolved to eradicate these divisions and put an end to the traditional tactics of imperialism of 'divide and rule,' which aim at pitting tribe against tribe, country against country, individual against individual. There was unfortunately too little said about economic problems in the speeches at the Conference, the emphasis almost throughout being on political emancipation. Nevertheless, many of the young delegates were thinking and talking privately about the dangers of continued imperialist exploitation in the newly indepen-

dent countries. They were very glad to have the question brought out into open discussion in the message which Dr. Du Bois sent to the Conference setting forth the choice which the liberated African people must make between the blandishments of a dying capitalism and the security and progress of the socialist way of life. Western imperialists, Dr. Du Bois warned, offer to let some of our smarter and less scrupulous leaders become fellow capitalists with the white exploiters if in turn they induce the nation's masses to pay the awful cost...Strive against it with every fibre of your bodies and souls. A body of local capitalists, even if they are black, can never free Africa; they will simply sell it into a new slavery to old masters overseas.

The conference stimulated Alphaeus tremendously, and he felt it marked an important new milestone in the liberation of the whole Africa. He met many African leaders whom he had know as students in the U.S. or their work in the U.N. He talked at length with Dr. Ivan Potekhin, one of the Soviet fraternal delegates to the conference, who was an authority on African history and Director of the Institute on African Studies in Moscow. Dr. Potekhin had spent some months in Ghana earlier and informed Alphaeus that his book had already been translated into Russian and would shortly be published in the Soviet Union by the Institute for Oriental Studies. The question of being invited to the Soviet Union was raised, and though Potekhin had no authority to invite him, he promised to see what he could do when he returned. Alphaeus's membership as a board member in the National Council of American-Soviet Friendship, he believed, would be helpful.

With constant running around writing articles and the excitement of trying to do and see too many things in Accra, he left his prized camera friends had given him in a taxi cab. Alphaeus was always losing something; usually it was his pipe, or umbrella, later in his travels he lost his gloves, scarf and several pens. "A half hour later," he wrote, "I was standing on the curb at a busy corner near where I had left the taxi, asking a policeman where to report the loss. Just then my taxi driver came running across the street holding the camera high in the air. He had been looking for me to return it. Wonderful, yes? That would hardly happen in New York. Well, I've been very careful since then." I doubt if he would be as lucky today. Times have changed considerably. Many African cities like those in America are plagued with thieves, and anything of value left in a taxi today would hardly be returned.

Alphaeus expressed to Kwame Nkrumah his eagerness to observe how the people lived and worked, and his desire to travel in Ghana. Nkrumah turned him over to someone in the Ministry of External Affairs, and he was thereafter treated as a guest of the Prime Minister. Before starting his Ghanaian tour, he took a dusty but interesting trip to Lome, Togoland, to visit Prime Minister Sylvanus E. Olympio. Olympio, a jolly, talkative man (who was later assassinated) was the first African to address the Trusteeship Council when he represented the All Ewe Conference in 1947. where he asked for Ewe unification, and an end of Anglo-French partition. It was during that visit that he and Rev. Michael Scott, of South Africa, who also attended the U.N. session in behalf of South-West African Affairs were our dinner guests.

On his return from Lome, Alphaeus left promptly for Ashanti and Northern territories. He was eager to visit the area where the remarkable Kingdom of Ashanti, The Gold Coast, once the most prosperous of pre-colonial Africa, flourished. Never dominated by the thrust of European demands, the Ashantians commanded armies that no neighboring power could match, and they fought no fewer than seven wars between 1806 and 1900, but were finally subdued by the British in 1901. A two week trip by bus through Kumasi, the Ashanti capital and lifeline of that intricate and lucrative empire, brought Alphaeus to Tamale and Navrongo near the northern border. There he was received by the local chief, whose heralds walked backward in front of him beating their drums as he approached his abode. Alphaeus preferred to travel by bus to see the country, much to the Minister's displeasure. One passed through village after village, often four or five in the space of two miles. Though traveling by government bus, which delivered mail and newspapers along the route, was slow, dirty and somewhat taxing, one viewed village life at a closer range, and he found it exceedingly engrossing.

"I was escorted to a spacious suite of rooms, all modern and spotless," Alphaeus wrote from Kumasi, "at the Residency of the Regional Commissioner (formerly the headquarters of the Chief Colonial Administrator in the area). All the luxury, elegance and servants have been retained from the colonial days...and a car at my disposal to go wherever I wish." It was the same thing all over again in Tamale, the capital of the Northern Territories, 237 miles from Kumasi. The Regional Commissioner and his wife were especially friendly and hospitable, and insisted that he return to Kumasi by car or plane and not by bus.

The second day in Lagos, Nigeria, Alphaeus met a Nigerian whom he knew in New York who was driving to Kano, a trip he planned to take by air. The opportunity of going by car was too tempting to ignore, and he invited himself along, much to the Nigerian's pleasure, as he did not relish the long trip unaccompanied. That gruelling 723-mile three-day trip was an unforgettable experience. Two-thirds of the route from Lagos to Kano was unsurfaced dirt road, and it was the dry season. One closed the car windows when another car approached in a swirl of dust, but still it would seep inside. Alphaeus described the discomforts:

> I wore shorts and a T-shirt during the trip and at the end of the day, I looked as if I had been in a coal mine. At one point we had to cross the Niger River. There was one narrow bridge, just wide enough for a single railroad track — everybody and everything had to cross this. We arrived just when some herds of cattle were crossing from the opposite side — we parked at the side and the animals, a couple of hundred, meandered past slowly, driven by herdsmen who on foot, guide, coax, whip and yell them along the way cross country from the cattle area in the North all the way to Lagos in the South where they are slaughtered (no wonder the beef is so stringy and tough). One poor cow fell down on the bridge and broke a leg and finally had to be hauled out of the way by a dozen men. Another thing you meet on the road were big trucks half filled with freight, and dusty-robed Moslems from the North, the human cargo occupying the rest of the space, as best they could. You'd see them climb down stiffly from the trucks at little villages, a sack of their possessions over their shoulders. And sometimes you'd pass a truck out of commission on the road-side—with the people sitting around waiting for who knows what, and there were some overturned and abandoned.

The big attraction in Kano is the thick-walled ancient city, the oldest section which stretches over several square miles and is constructed of mud and recoated year after year. There, only Moslems are allowed to live behind the partly crumbled walls with their twelve massive gates, and a maze of winding, narrow streets. Kano has a history dating back at least a thousand years when it was a caravan crossroads in medieval times, and continues to be a busy trading center. The residents are heavily robed against the windborne dust that hangs like a fog in the distance. Few women are seen on the gritty streets, as Kano women are kept well hidden from the gaze of outsiders. After centuries of servitude and submissiveness, the long neglected Moslem girls are breaking out of their traps. The people in the north are more backward than the rest of Nigeria and you find few educated young men outside the upper crust of feudal ruling families, who send their sons to Oxford or Cambridge, never to the U.S.

While walking out alone, his first day in Kano, Alphaeus met a bright young lad who offered to show him around and suggested that hey rent bicycles — sixpence an hour. Off they went, sightseeing in the old walled city, ducking between autos, cattle and pedestrians. As if that was not enough, that seat of Alphaeus's bike kept slipping out of place. He eventually tied it down after scraping against a man's car and suffering a shocked and indignant stare. Nevertheless, they peddled around for two hours and he considered the tour well worthwhile.

Dr. Nnamdi Azikiwe, then Premier of Eastern Nigeria, knew of Alphaeus's coming to Enugu, and he was met at the airport and taken to the Catering Rest House as Azikiwe was out of town. The C.R.H. (as it was called) serves mainly Europeans traveling or working in the area. It is run by the government, and such houses are found in all major towns. They are very comfortable bungalow quarters with private bath, central dining room, and other services similar to those of a hotel, but the charge is considerably less.

Alphaeus visited coal mines, where everyone received him warmly, and he talked to some of the miners and their wives, explaining how the Council on African Affairs had raised funds for their relief at the time of their big strike in 1949.

Dr. Azikiwe returned to the city for a few hours the day before he left, and although there were many people to see him (including the Ghana Commissioner who came from Kano on the same plane with Alphaeus), he would see no one except Alphaeus. "We talked for nearly an hour," Alphaeus commented, "despite his promise of only five minutes. Azikiwe seemed genuinely glad to see me and have a chance to talk frankly about some of the serious problems he faces."

Azikiwe, Nigeria's first and only President from 1963 to 1966, was a chief architect of Nigeria's independence from Britain. He had written Alphaeus a very warm letter (after reading his book twice), in which he said:

> ...Because you have been through the crucible, and know what it means to be a man of conviction, I will always doff my hat to you. There are not many people of your ilk in the world today, and I feel that men like you need to know that in spite of the odds that are stacked against you, there is at least one corner of the world where your efforts are appreciated.
>
> I want you to stand firm in the cause of righteousness, because your sacrifice has been an inspiration to those of us who are now impervious to all sorts of victimization and ostracisation. You know that

in the end it will yield the fruit of satisfaction, and that is why some of us have been in the struggle for over a quarter of a century.

At times, we may appear to have fallen by the wayside, but if you were here in Africa and see the role of ignorance, poverty and superstition, you will blame us less for not transforming our deserts into a rich and fertile field overnight.

On his last full day in Enugu, Alphaeus motored to Onitsha, a major trading center on the Niger River. With hundreds of others he was quickly swallowed up in a noisy crowd elbowing each other along good naturedly in one of the biggest markets in West Africa. Thousands of stalls and stands cover several square miles and an amazing variety of merchandise is displayed both locally and imported. The persistent hawking of one friendly trader caused him to stop and admire the popular Kola nuts neatly spread out on a mat. The trader's animated sales talk made not the slightest impact. Not to be outdone, he pressed a nut in his hand, begging him to try the kernel that gave one a "life."

One day in Onitsha was quite enough for Alphaeus, and he moved on to Ibadan where he visited the new University College, then the largest and most advanced African University (with close to a thousand students) situated in the most spacious city in all black Africa between Johannesburg and Cairo. The University was modern in structure, and Alphaeus thought it was "somewhat on the luxurious style, for dormitories, for faculty homes and for visitors' quarters." Many of the young faculty members with whom he talked were extremely critical of the British domination of the school, and commented that a class of pampered, elite Africans, separated from their people, was being developed there. They pointed out, for example, that the library had not a single Nigerian newspaper, nor any other African papers — only British dailies. They knew, however, that many things would be changed when Nigeria became independent in 1960.

Alphaeus fortunately reached the old Yoruba city, Ife, in time for the agricultural fair, always an enlivening event. Ife is famous for its beautiful bronze heads and figures that sculptors produced more than a thousand years ago in honor of their kings. Part of the fair program was a series of colorful and exciting traditional dances, accompanied by drums and other native instruments; something he had not yet seen anywhere in his travels.

Back in Lagos, our Nigerian friend "Ladi" (Olandio Onipede) took Alphaeus in hand. Onipede was the principal of the largest school in Lagos, Lagos Municipal College, a private institution owned by Azikiwe, whose militant newspaper lit the torch of freedom that flashed across the

Gold Coast. Alphaeus spoke to the assembly of students in the seatless assembly hall, where the girls stood in front, the boys behind, very disciplined and quiet. Later when he talked to the teachers, "the discussion was so prolonged, " he said, "they asked so many questions, that Ladi had to break it up to get classes going. It was one of the most memorable mornings in Africa."

Ladi put the school bus, used for getting teachers to and from school, at Alphaeus's disposal for two hours a day, to cruise around town — a considerable saving in taxi fares. He did a great deal of exploring on foot, and alone. Lagos, a hot, humid, crowded city where traffic jams are impenetrable, and the moist aroma of open drains competes with the blistering sun that makes you wringing wet in fifteen minutes, is an island like Manhattan. One must cross a bridge to reach the mainland, and there lies the crux of the traffic problem, aggravated by the steady mass movement from the rural area to the already overcrowded, unhealthy slums.

Alphaeus met and talked with a number of labor and political leaders, including the preeminent woman leader in the country, Mrs. Funmilayo Ransone-Kuti. Several who were in government or business remembered him as editor of **Spotlight on Africa**, which they had read.

The commitments made to send articles home were difficult to fulfill. He was concerned that constant travel — much of it by car, and lack of time to settle down in any one place long enough to write or even collect his thoughts — had prevented him from dispatching many news items on Ghana and Nigeria. Alphaeus thought it necessary to use the time seeing and absorbing as much as possible, deferring the writing until later when he hoped to have a few free days.

Alphaeus found Guinea quite different, as there was no African middle class elite. "There's something else that makes me hesitate about coming to Nigeria or Ghana to settle down at the present time," he wrote from Conakry, the capital of Guinea. "With some notable exceptions here and there, those in influential positions in government or university circles tend towards being a snobbish, high-living elite class with too little real concern about the welfare and advancement of the whole nation. Liberia, of course, is the classic example of that, and Ghana and Nigeria are not as bad as Liberia by any means but they do manifest the same fatal tendencies at the present time."

The government leaders like Sekou Touré, the President , are mostly trade union leaders by background, and Guinea, unlike the other French territories, stood for no nonsense from De Gaulle and his constitution — but chose independence. Alphaeus found no luxurious living, except at the European hotel, a relic of colonial days, where he stayed as a guest of the government, simply because they had nowhere else to house their guest.

"There are no showy government buildings, residences or government cars available for guests here," he continued, "and only six taxis (which charge exorbitantly) in the city, so you do a good deal of walking. In terms of the intellectual climate, I would prefer to live and work here. But there's one drawback, alas — my lack of savvy in French."

In Guinea, Alphaeus received the same kind of V.I.P. treatment as in Ghana — but with a difference. His hotel room was expensive, and he could not have stayed there on his own. He didn't like the idea of adding his hotel bill, relatively small though it was, to the financial problems of the government that the four-month-old country had to face. He felt a little uncomfortable in all that luxury, and he was glad to leave after his short stay soon after his interview on the radio ended.

For a tourist, trying to cope with a foreign language, the effort can be both frustrating and stimulating. For Alphaeus, he "never felt so utterly stupid and helpless," as during his last days in Africa, visiting Guinea and Abidjan, on the Ivory Coast. Pressed by dire necessity, he began to recall some of the French he had once studied. Though he had little difficulty reading French, understanding the spoken word was something else. At least he mastered numbers and knew how much something cost when one quoted a price. He decided then to learn French conversation — without delay, when he returned.

In Abidjan, he visited the Director of Education, who took him to several primary schools and the Lycee (preparatory to college) where the director in charge was very cordial, and curious about American education. Both Frenchmen spoke some English, fortunately. The Lycee director voiced his concern about the discipline of the African students. "In France," he said, "when you discipline a student, he bowed respectfully and accepted his punishment; but here, whenever you try to discipline these Africans, regardless of their age (about 12 to 18), they would all talk about "Dignité! Dignité!" Alphaeus informed the director that it was a logical consequence of colonialism, and the only remedy was to recruit African teachers, to take over as quickly as possible. There was only one African on the faculty and he was leaving to go into politics.

Thanks to the directions given him by the Lycee director, Alphaeus found his way to a remarkable dwelling -- the Bungerville School of Art, conducted by an old Frenchman in the bush country off a dirt road about ten miles outside Abidjan. He lived there for over twenty years without ever leaving. Africans initiated him into fetish rituals, and he would be killed if he tried to leave.

The eighteen students who live and work there stay for five years; some go for further study to Paris. "There was one house for students and himself (he had no family)," Alphaeus said, "and another large high-ceilinged shed where they did wood carving. In the back of the shed in an alcove, artfully illuminated by partly shaded electric lights, that he calls his museum, here the finished works are displayed." The most wonderful African wood sculpture of contemporary style that he had ever seen anywhere—giant, larger than life size heads, torsos and whole figures in beautifully grained wood. The style was alive, vibrant, not static--one figure for instance, was a man with face lifted up and mouth open singing. The teacher, a kindly, slender white haired man in his seventies or eighties, understood no English, nor did anyone else there, and Alphaeus struggled the best he could with his feeble French. He was the first American ever to visit the school. Though he couldn't buy anything, he was very pleased with himself at having found the hideout and to have viewed such remarkable work. "This is certainly one place we **must** revisit together," he wrote.

After two exciting months in Africa, Alphaeus visited our friend, Helen Hagen Wilga, in Florence; spent three days in Rome, and four in Paris, where Ollie Harrington, noted cartoonist for the **Pittsburgh Courier** and author of the book **Bootsie and Others** shepherded him around. His letters were full of excitement, always ending. "We must come back and see this together."

From hot, sunny Africa to cold, rainy England was not an inviting and comfortable change in late February. Alphaeus was eager to reach London to find news, if any, of the hoped for invitation to the Soviet Union. Meantime, at home, friends planned a tour of the U.S.S.R. and I longed to join the group; but I hesitated to strip my savings, knowing full well that Alphaeus had no job and no prospects of one. Feeling sorry for myself, I reread some of his letters with vivid accounts of his activities, and for the first time I realized that it was the house that possessed me instead of my possessing the house. I quickly decided to go.

Alphaeus was disappointed not to find a letter from Dr. Potekhin when he arrived in London. He knew of my decision to take the tour and he was delighted and restless to join me in Amsterdam, our first stop. A few consultations at the Soviet Embassy, however, started the wheels of progress to turn, and the invitation finally arrived after a month and a half of anxiety, much to our relief and joy.

Several notable events brightened the weeks of uneasy waiting; foremost among them was the opening performance of "Othello" at Stratford-on-Avon. A ticket from Paul Robeson enabled Alphaeus to enjoy his magnificent performance; the house had been sold out for weeks, and an opening night ticket could not be had for any price.

To save money that dwindled fast, the expected meeting in Amsterdam did not occur. Alphaeus, instead, took a boat from London to Gothenburg, Sweden, a train to Stockholm, then a boat to Helsinki (our second stop), and was on hand, radiant with happiness, as I stepped off the plane. We flew to Leningrad the following day, and celebrated our sixteenth wedding anniversary.

With only four days at our disposal, we saw just a few of the fascinating places of interest in that beautiful, historical city of nearly six hundred bridges lacing the metropolis. Some called Leningrad the Venice of the North, but Venice never boasted such a spacious highway as Nevsky Prospect. One could easily spend an entire week merely browsing through the regal State Hermitage with its exquisite treasury of art, heirlooms of a turbulent and splendid past, and still not cover the entire museum, of a thousand rooms, which was once the winter palace of Czar Nicholas II and Alexandria.

A representative of the Academy of Sciences visited Alphaeus soon after our arrival to discuss plans for his stay. We anticipated a rich and stimulating experience in that stalwart nation. No people in the history of battle ever suffered more than the Soviet Union during four years of strife in World War II.

A visit with Professor D. A. Olderrege, of Leningrad University, an expert on Arabic languages and culture and head of the Institute of Oriental Studies, gave Alphaeus a chance to discuss with him at length some facets of African history they had touched upon through correspondence.

To witness the May 1st celebration in Moscow's Red Square is a thrilling, exciting spectacle, to say the least. Thousands of young people represented a vast and varied domain with its mixture of races who speak, perhaps a hundred languages and dialects, and whose racial and cultural origins emanate from a number of civilizations.

As we scrutinized the gilded, onion-shaped domes of the cathedrals that mutely overlook the Kremlin, Moscow's apex of power, we realized how ancient the city is. Enclosed by a massive brick and stone wall, the Kremlin is a complex of churches and palaces from medieval times; but the palaces have been converted into government offices, congress halls, a theater and museum.

The absence of a fare collector on our first streetcar ride struck us as odd. Only a change box was visible. The government apparently put you on your honor. "Reading seems to be the national pastime," Alphaeus remarked, as we observed many young people deeply engrossed in their books in public. Contemporary popular literature as well as new editions of the great Russian classics are snapped up overnight. Though nowhere today are books printed in such quantities as in the Soviet Union, they have difficulty meeting demands.

Stores were filled with merchandise, though waiting lines stretched out and brought fatigue to many, whose faces, etched with the telltale marks of war gave silent evidence of years of struggle, deprivation and strife. The constant strain to survive, by superhuman effortrs had exhausted the people and taken its toll. Yet, conditions were improving.

105

As guest of the Academy of Sciences, and royalties from Alphaeus's book, every day brought new encounters. Between his conferences, speeches, and a radio talk, we took a boat to the old city, Sukumi, visited the calm, green-blue Lake Ritsa, high in the Ukraine mountains, and other sights. But the week's rest at Sochi, the beautiful summer resort on the Black Sea, where thousands of workers take their yearly vacations in one of the palatial rest homes, topped them all.

After a month of constant activity with new found friends whose warmth and hospitality made our visit a memorable event, we departed for Poland.

The Academy of Sciences in Warsaw, our host, had several outings planned, and Alphaeus met with two members of the Academy. The most unforgettable day for him was the visit to Chopin's birthplace, Zelazowa-Wola. The composer's home sits in a quiet, scenic panorama of luxuriant gardens, where snow white swans glide sedately on the smooth, clear pond, seemingly swaying to the soft, sweet melodies of the unhappy Chopin, as they floated through the open window.

Every Sunday a concert of Chopin's music was given, and always to an overflowing crowd, including many children and young people, who enjoyed his dulcet sonatas while sitting on the grass. After a week we left for the charming, old city Prague, Czechoslovkia.

Alphaeus greeted his good friend, George Wheeler, with gusto at the airport. Wheeler, an American economist, settled in Prague with his wife Eleanor and four children during the early years of the McCarthy era. Soon Alphaeus had his map in hand, determined to fill our seven days to the brim, with a list of all the places we must see. Nothing gave him more pleasure than exploring a city by streetcar or bus, visiting the most unlikely districts, and seeing a great deal of Prague which we otherwise would not have seen.

In Paris, he followed the same procedure. Two months of constant going, however, had taken the wind out of my sails, and I wanted to do nothing but **sit**. Not he. Bright and early we were off on the Metro to one spot—or "hoofing" it to another, until another week passed. At the end of a restful weekend with our friends Edita and Ira Morris in the quietness of their home and garden outside of Paris, Alphaeus suggested that we go to Switzerland. "We might as well see as much as we can while we're over here," he said. "We may never have the chance again."

That excursion took us to Geneva, Interlaken and Lucerne with stops in Rome, Venice, and Florence. By bus, horse and buggy and train, we saw many of Italy's beauty spots including Capri, Sorrento, Naples and Pompeii.

The highlight of the trip came when we attended (as guests) the Seventh World Youth Festival in Vienna, July 26 - August 4th. Vienna, a city as ageless as its songs, is one of the world's great tourist centers. Though much has been done to modernize the city, the past still claims it as its own.

Homeward bound at last, one more **must** still remained, "Othello." Checking in at a small hotel in London, late at night we nevertheless started out almost at the crack of dawn for Stratford-on-Avon.

·The beauty and hushed tranquility of that quaint English village, with its breathless simplicity, made a lasting impression on Alphaeus. We had precious little time to explore before the performance, and took a train back to London immediately after it ended. Yet, what little we saw, the calm flowing of the river Avon and lush greenery of many varieties, where we sat for some time, brought to our tired bodies a measure of restful relaxation from its aura of natural serenity.

Eight months of intensive travel for Alphaeus and four for me had come to an end. Weary and exhausted but filled with joy and happiness, we arrived in New York grateful for the marvelous opportunity to make such an exciting trip which added immeasurably to our understanding and knowledge of another section of the human family miles across the sea.

Sochi, U.S.S.R., 1959

Dr. Nnamdi Azikiwe
Premier of Eastern Nigeria, 1959

Alphaeus, Prof. D.A. Olderogge of Leningrad University, an expert in Arabic language culture, 1959

Palace of Pioneers, Leningrad, U.S.S.R., 1959

Leaving for Africa, May 1960

Relaxing in the sun at Sochi, U.S.S.R., 1959

Alphaeus and interpreter, U.S.S.R., 1959

Leningrad, U.S.S.R., 1959

Alphaeus, Shirley Du Bois, Kwame Nkrumah, Eslanda Robeson
Government House, Ghana, Dec. 1958

9. GUINEA: A NEW CAREER

Though constraining forces had stopped Joseph McCarthy's ruthless rampage when we returned, the hypnotic appeal of his idea that held thousands in fear had not weakened. Nor had the wheels of government that skidded so easily to a halt during his reign been steered onto a democratic course. McCarthyism still lived.

Alphaeus's prospects for the future in terms of employment remained as bleak as before. He knew the smouldering embers displayed a warning, a familiar method of reaction to denounce every democratic action as subversive, and then use the accusation as an alibi for its destruction. Years of frustration and longing deepened and widened Alphaeus's outlook, leaving no trace of bitterness or rancor within.

Speaking engagements on his African journey, however, afforded an opportunity to rise slightly above an otherwise depressing situation. Alphaeus firmly believed no power on earth would be able to silence the voice of Africa. "The leaders of today's struggles," he reminded an alert audience, "are the heirs of great African heroes of the past who fought to prevent the conquest of their people by the European invaders. They represent a tradition and are on the road to re-establishing the status of Africans as free men. Today, the struggle for peace and the struggle for colonial liberation are one, and peace and freedom are invincible." He expressed the hope that the emerging countries would realize that their strength resided in their diversities including varied historical backgrounds. A new force in a new world had appeared.

With each passing season the intense struggle for total African freedom grew sharper, and in 1960 Alphaeus revised **Decision in Africa** with a new postscript. He continued research for a second book on the problems of economic development in the new independent African states. He set his heart on returning to Africa. There, he thought he could make a better contribution. "Sunlight, joy and peace," he wrote me many years before,

"—it's good to enjoy these things, but even while enjoying them it is necessary not to forget the everlasting battle against hate, prejudice, oppression and darkness of ignorance. One feels pleasure (or pain) as an individual," he continued, "but one must live and think and act as a fragment of all humanity or of one's community or any group that has one common objective."

Alphaeus did not think it possible to live entirely as an individual, as some believed. "The joy and strength of cooperative group activity and effort, the concept of Christian brotherhood — all these things," he said, "prove that man is essentially a social being."

In January 1960, for the first time in months of despondency, his depressed spirits received a boost by an invitation from President Sekou Toure of Guinea to teach in the Lycee, prior to serving as professor of English in the university being established. The Guinean Ambassador to the U.S., Diallo Telli, whom Alphaeus knew, had paved the way.

The Guinean government, aware that illiteracy is the enemy of democracy, planned rapid development of higher educational services for the masses whom the French deliberately maintained in darkness. Touré knew that wherever the standard of education is low the standard of living is low, and he proposed to change the shocking condition. It was one of the government's many instances of outstanding progress since independence. Hitherto, Guineans were compelled to go to Paris or Dakar for higher studies. Also significant in terms of Pan African unity was the new attention to instruction in English on all levels, together with French, the official language.

Alphaeus tingled at the thought of returning to Africa, the wettest and dryest of continents. He hoped it would be possible to continue writing in conjunction with teaching duties. His principle concern never centered on himself or on security, but on the interest and worthwhileness of his work in the current of life rushing past him. As there appeared no way out of the continued, miasmic circumstances forced upon him in the United States, wherever a door opened for him, I intended to go.

Despite weeks of excitement and activity in preparation for our departure, mixed emotions occasionally filled my mind while dismantling our home. Starting a new life in a strange land created disturbing thoughts at times, but the knowledge that "home is where the heart is," quickly overshadowed the brief, uncertain periods.

The African sun, undimmed by any clouds, held sway with its blazing brilliance when we landed in Conakry, the capital of Guinea, in May of 1960, though it was barely eight o'clock. The most mountainous country in West Africa with four geographical divisions, Guinea is a land of wide diversity of climate and customs. The middle section, Fouta-Djallon, rises from three to five thousand feet above sea level, and offers one of the most healthful climates in Africa. Its air is cool and dry, unlike Conakry, in the lower coastal area where the hot, humid atmosphere plays havoc with one's strength.

To be again in that throbbing continent in the throes of transition brought a touch of excitement to Alphaeus as he talked to our host of the peoples' ambitious hopes; their feverish desires to hasten progress at breakneck speed. They were determined to forge a position of prominence in the industrial world; a position denied them by forced colonial practices designed specifically to keep the African territories producing agricultural products exclusively for the colonial powers. With their bewildering array of customs, tribes, and languages, Alphaeus knew full well the future would present strange contrast and contradictions.

Our small hotel in the heart of a suburb of Conakry stood on the corner of a busy intersection. It faced a huge African market, under a wide-open sky, and a beehive of activity pervaded the place from sun up to sundown. The striking colors and flowing lines of the women's gowns and exquisite artistry with which they festooned their heads with matching or contrasting colors gave a dazzling effect against their dark skin. Watching a mother quickly swing her baby on her back, wrap a piece of cloth around it, tie it securely, and briskly walk down the street balancing numerous articles on her head intrigued us. The vivid panorama of that ceaseless activity soon came to an abrupt end, however, when we moved into an apartment on the campus of Lycee Donka.

We found life in Guinea, to some extent rough: consumer goods were in short supply, many food staples were scarce. Those available were extremely high. Locally produced fruits were plentiful and cheap. With no car, no refrigerator and no gas for our stove, preparing a single-dish meal during the first month proved a frustrating ordeal. It required taxiing to the city every day to make fresh purchases. To make matters worse, one had to pump vigorously on a small oil burner to light the wick, which occasionally wouldn't light at all. Finally, after two months, our precious belongings arrived, and that called for an evening's celebration with friends.

Alphaeus once wrote, "One of the good things about being in Guinea was the feeling that one was in the mainstream not only of African liberation forces but what was progressive globally." The weekend Patrice Lumumba, Prime Minister of the Congo, visited Conakry on his way home to the Congo (Zaire) contributed to one of the most thrilling of our nearly three months' residence. The city's welcome turned into a gala event. Though the Congolese were tragically unprepared for independence, they were aflame with the burning desire to rule themselves.

The town's populace solidly lined the entire route from the airport to the President's residence in the city, some ten miles. On one side stood all the

115

male Africans, bare-footed five year old boys to venerable patriarchs in white robes and leather sandals and carrying white umbrellas. On the other side all the girls and women, many with babies on their backs, attired in their festive best. The women lightened the long wait for the honored guest by songs and dances (the men only watched and applauded) to the accompaniment of drums, native xylophonic instruments, and rhythmic clapping.

Lumumba unquestionably enjoyed the widest support among his countrymen. His brutal assassination in 1961 touched off a fistswinging fracas by American Blacks in the United Nations gallery. This made headlines in Africa when they marched through the streets of New York shouting "Congo, Yes! Yankee, No!" Black youths, frustrated by years of racism, identified the rise of Black Africa and its battles for freedom with their own constant struggle for equality in the U.S. Jail no longer held fear, and many considered it an honor to go behind bars for the Congo as for decent housing in Harlem to bring into reality the ideals so loudly proclaimed by the nation to all the world but denied to many at home.

Alphaeus kept his friends and colleagues in the States informed by newsletters and articles of the rapid pace of events surrounding us. As Associate Editor of **Freedomways,** he wrote "Guinea Strides Forward" for the first issue in 1961, in which he depicts some of the problems and achievements of that newly independent country. Almost weekly a succession of economic and cultural missions from many countries arrived. Delegations of youth, women and workers came from the Soviet Union and the German Democratic Republic. The Chinese acrobats from the People's Republic of China thought nothing of going to remote villages in the dense bush to perform their intricate tricks, to the joy and delight of the peasants, and they caused a sensation wherever they performed.

At the conclusion of the Third World Congress of Teachers in Conakry, in the Hall of the People, the audience witnessed a hair-raising display of masterly drumming. Alphaeus had tried to explain the emotional impact it aroused in him during his African tour, but it defies description. To an outsider, you try, if possible, to catch the true meaning as you watch the changing expressions and intense feelings reflected in the drummers' perspiring faces as strong, hard hands pound the giant drums. They are, indeed, "talking drums," shaped like an hourglass, "the oldest human sounds in Africa," sending messages and telling stories with their surprising range of tonal qualities to all who have ears to hear. It is not so much the element of sound that bewitches you, as powerful as that is, but the rhythm that gradually pervades the senses and excites the nerves, making it almost impossible to remain still. Alphaeus brought his tape recorder, and had taped half of Touré's speech when the tape gave out, much to his annoyance, and in trying to change it he lost a screw, which put an end to the taping.

Labor bodies all over the country voted to donate their labor instead of taking Saturday afternoons off for three or four months in the interest of the success of the national effort. On Sundays too (Guinea is predominately Moslem) flag-bedecked trucks of gay youngsters drove by on their way to some volunteer road-repair or construction job. Throughout the country the campaign which everyone spoke of as "human investment," gathered momentum. Workers, farmers, women and youth assisted the government in building hundreds of new schools, health centers, markets and other structures, and in the clearing and cultivation of vast new areas of land.

Although the population of Conakry had jumped considerably since independence, reflecting the movement city-ward, visible in varying degrees everywhere in Africa, Guineans remained .a rural, agricultural people. The government concentrated, therefore, on raising the level of life and productivity in the countryside, where ninety percent of the people lived and worked. A more formidable task in Alphaeus' opinion, called for the education of an entire nation to recognition of their great responsibility in making the Three Year Plan of Economic Development work.

We saw also some depressing sights: boys and old men with misshapen bodies begging; able-bodied men with nothing more to do than peddle cigarettes, matches, and cola nuts, or just stand around idly; the waste of manpower on jobs that should be done by machine; over-manned and poorly organized offices.

Things can move with agonizing slowness in Africa. It required seven trips to one department for Alphaeus to get his first salary. Those conditions were, of course, in large part the residue of colonialism, which did more damage to the coastal towns like Conakry than in the areas less penetrated by European influences. He soon realized that the task of decolonization in the sense of changing men's habits of thought and action demanded more than persuasion in the former centers of colonial administration and commerce.

The legacy of poverty, disease and illiteracy existed in Guinea as in the rest of Africa, Alphaeus noted, and, "one could see in the streets of Conakry the effects of the criminal waste and degradation of human life." Yet, there was an important difference along the city's business streets; there was none of the shocking contrast of opulence and misery so prevalent in other cities he visited. No fancy luxury-goods shops catering exclusively to a wealthy bourgeoisie, for no such class of either foreigners or Africans exists in Guinea.

Though Guinea is potentially the richest in all French Africa, along with almost unlimited water power, her tremendously large deposits of aluminum bauxite constitute the main export despite her wealth in diamonds, gold, nickel, chrome and iron. The untapped resources of this great wealth have no value, however, until dams can be built to harness the waiting water-power.

Alphaeus describes in **Decision in Africa** how some chiefs were used as servants of the colonial officials, thus working against the interest of their people, and perpetuating feudal barriers to the development of political democracy. The Democratic Party of Guinea (D.P.G.) succeeded in having the institution of chiefs officially abolished before independence — another respect in which Guinea was unique among African states. The leaders realized that no nation, society or individual can really progress while clinging to precedent and the hide-bound, encrusted traditions of the past. The land held by the chiefs became state property, which neither could be bought nor sold or converted into hired-labor plantations.

Improvement of farming techniques received much attention, Alphaeus observed, during a trip to the interior. Experts from China and elsewhere demonstrated better methods of growing rice and other crops, and modern tools were brought in to replace the back-breaking dabas (a short hoe). Old habits die slowly, and many veteran farmers, bent from years of its usage, were still reluctant to try modern tools.

By the end of August, torrential rain descended on the city, loosening and lifting the hard, baked earth and washing away huge quantities of top soil, leaving a parched, eroded surface. Guinea has only two seasons — dry and rainy, and Conakry gets nearly twelve feet of rain a year, with the harmattan, a dry, dust-laden land wind from the Sahara, thrown in for good measure.

Alphaeus insisted that we get some relaxation and a change from constant downpour before school opened in October. A four week trip to Lagos and back by boat supplied the answer, with a brief stop-over in Abidjan and Accra. Embarking we had our first glimpse of how the poor, harassed Africans travel. They came with every conceivable kind of luggage, including chickens, and their berths for the night would be the deck, regardless of the weather. It was an ill-fated journey.

Our first night out, an incident on shipboard symbolized the cross-currents then sweeping Africa. In the dining salon (third class) a violent argument arose between some African passengers and the French steward and waiters. The latter wanted the Africans to hold their small children in their laps instead of occupying seats at the table. The Africans protested, and pointed across the salon to the French families whose children were sitting in their own chairs, and said they were not going to stand for any discrimination. The ship's chief steward finally made his appearance, accompanied by a towering African assistant. The African passengers were not impressed; they argued all the louder for their rights. Subsequently, the chief steward went into a huddle with his assistant and the salon steward, and the assistant assured the aggrieved that everything would be all right. For the rest of the voyage the black children, too, had their own seats and all was calm.

At two of the tables sat African soldiers on leave from service with the French army in Algeria and on their way to their homes in Dahomey, Ivory Coast and French Congo. During the fracas, we noticed that they kept their eyes fixed steadily on their plates and said not a word. It was as though they existed in another world.

The end of our enjoyable interlude turned into disaster on our last night in Lagos. While we slept, a prowler made off with both our wrist watches, Alphaeus' treasured camera, a goodly sum of U.S. money, which we had held in reserve for emergencies, and a big valise full of clothes and other effects all packed and ready for our departure the next morning. We recovered nothing and it compelled me to borrow clothes to make the trip. A devastating experience to initiate us into our new African life.

Before school opened, Alphaeus discussed with the President how best to contribute his services. He offered assistance in a course on Foreign Affairs at Ecole National with the possible topics of **United Nations and African Administration; United States Policy in Africa and Problems of Pan-African Unity and Co-operation.** He also wanted to assist in preparation of a new English edition of President Touré's writings and speeches. Unfortunately, those projects did not materialize before our unexpected departure.

Although Alphaeus disliked more than ever the exhaustion of teaching, which he thought he had securely put behind him, he nevertheless did willingly whatever he could to help the toiling nation. He believed that a successful teacher is inspired with love of his pupils, and since he never did anything by halves, he threw himself into his work ungrudgingly, even taking on the added job of preparing and giving English language news broadcasts for Radio Conakry. He eventually had to relinquish that task as the hectic deadlines of translations deprived him of too much time needed for his school work.

Students from all over Guinea came to Lycee Donka, which comprised Lycee Classique and Lycee Technique, and their ages ranged from fourteen to eighteen. The government provided for all their needs during their schooling; lodging, meals, minimum clothing, including a plastic raincoat, textbooks and exercise books, even ballpoint pens. Though it was easier to provide more buildings than to find badly needed teachers for the rapidly growing school population, there were forty nationalities represented among the new teachers that year. Virtually all important European and some Asian countries had teachers in Guinea; many came from the Caribbean and the United States.

In Lycee Classique, where Alphaeus taught, he noted some progress toward re-orientating the content of the various courses toward African rather than European experiences and interest, but not nearly enough. In his English courses they still used text-books portraying the life of upper middle class European children. That annoyed him no end, and as a beginning, to remedy the situation, he made a selection of scores of passages of African and Black American writings and had them mimeographed for translation practice.

The students were hungry for information about African countries, and Black Americans in particular. When Alphaeus brought a few copies of the **Afro-American** newspaper and had the students read aloud about Castro in Harlem, Nkrumah and Touré, new African members of the U.N., and Black sports stars, they almost smothered him with questions, and fought to get possession of the papers at the end of class.

He consistently tried to bring interesting materials to the students' attention, and at the request of the Minister of Education, he headed a committee of teachers charged with the revision of the English methods of instruction and the selection of new and more relevant material.

He thought the classes more disciplined and devoted to more serious study than in most American high schools. "I'm sure the average student here learns English far more thoroughly than the average student there learns French or another foreign language," he wrote to a high school teacher in New York, who had complained about his pupils' deplorable compositions.

He was keenly aware, more often than not, that many students who reached a high educational level became completely isolated from the society of their rearing, and took a narrow, shortsighted view of education. Some wanted only a successful career, others a substantial income; still others desired an entree into society. Africa's new developing countries, Alphaeus told his students, could ill afford such selfish actions from those the government educated at terrific cost.

On the contrary, aside from the individual's self-fulfillment, he should be oriented to the needs of society's members and not alienate himself from the world beyond the campus. He warned that once the educated man burnt the bridge between himself and society, the task of rebuilding is indeed difficult. The future progress of Africa depended on the student of today, he reminded them. They had a responsibility to Guinea to give back to the people the fruits of their knowledge.

Besides English and French, Arabic was also a required subject — all in the interest of African unity. The Guinean students, on the whole, carried a very heavy study schedule, and had little time for frivolity. Nevertheless, they displayed an avid interest in sports.

After many years' experience as a skilled dressmaker and instructor in that craft in New York City schools, I intended to share that knowledge with the young Guinean women. When the Minister of Education asked me to teach English, in the girls' school adjacent to the Lycee, my heart sank. The school had a dressmaking teacher. That year it became a professional training school where students would no longer learn home economics and allied courses, but all the necessary skills to become a good secretary, an almost non-existent phenomenon in Guinea. English was now compulsory. I told the Minister that I had never taught English. He smiled and said quietly, "You can teach, can't you?" That was that! No one else was available. I was drafted.

My pupils consisted of the entire school, two hundred girls in ten classes. It was one thing to speak English, but quite another to teach it. Aside from having to study my horrible French every day, to keep one day ahead, (if that) of my classes in lessons and rules required unrelenting diligence. Alphaeus helped wonderfully, disciplining me as though I sat in his class, and patiently guided me through the maze of tests and lesson plans that never seemed to end. With that tight schedule, and supervising the work of our cook steward and teaching him how to read and write, and helping two young teachers (Russian and Vietnamese) with their English, my days were full to overflowing.

Teaching teenagers presented a challenge as my experience had been only with mature night-school students eager to learn. They wasted no time getting down to business. Now, when forty energetic freshmen of various ages confronted me my first day, I knew I was not ready for them. I also knew that class discipline would cease if they realized my dilemma.

After trying for a half-hour, without much success, to get some semblance of order, I started gathering my books and paper from my desk. I had not come to Guinea, I said, to waste my time and the government's money. If they were not interested in learning, I would leave immediately and go teach others who were. As I started walking towards the door, bedlam broke out; the entire class jumped up, surrounded me imploring me not to leave, and promising better conduct.

Despite hardships and frequent harassment, teaching at the Secretariat provided a rewarding and stimulating experience. It tested my patience, understanding and ability to relate to the African students, who felt close to me as the only Black teacher in the school. **The Teacher's Creed** Alphaeus wrote more than twenty years before came into sharp focus. For the first time, I understood that nobody is in a better position than the teacher to shape young minds. The teacher's role reaches far beyond the subjects taught, and his or her powers and responsibilities often condition the quality of a person's future in society.

One hot, humid day, at the end of a trying week, a young pupil came up to my desk after class, stood there a moment looking nervously at first one thing, then another, and said, "Madam, please give me a franc." Exhausted from a week of tests and annoyed by a student's pranks in the class just dismissed, I answered her rather sharply, ending with, "Why do you ask me? I'm not your mother!"

She looked up suddenly, surprised, her big, black eyes glistening with tears.

"But you **are** my mother," she said.

My embarrassment knew no bounds. Shocked and ashamed, I wanted to crawl under the desk and hide. Realizing my devastating mistake, I quickly took her shaking body in my arms, and tried to soothe her fears, telling her I was, indeed her mother. Though I had no children of my own, all children were mine because I was a universal mother, but if I gave her a franc, others would expect the same. Soon she dried her tears, and a warm smile spread over her face as she released my hand and said goodbye.

Our lives continued with feverish activity, but the Easter holidays brought a short respite, making Alphaeus unwilling to linger in Conakry during the break. A trip to Freetown, the capital of Sierra Leone (some forty miles by air from Conakry), afforded a needed tonic to our tired minds and weak bodies. We especially appreciated the leisurely strolls on the beach, with sand so white and fine one wanted to caress it. Unlike the small beach in Conakry filled with rocks and always crowded, this one, as far as the eye could see, was empty and we enjoyed the serenity of watching the waves break into bubbling foam and rush headlong over our bare feet.

Freetown in many respects resembled a poor Black community in the southern U.S. The peoples' dress and way of life differed markedly from Conakry, and for a good reason. The British abolitionists purchased land there for resettlement of liberated slaves in 1787, and the area became a British protectorate. Not to be outdone, the American Colonization Society, an abolitionist group, secured an adjoining area for the resettlement of slaves freed in America in 1821, and the Republic of Liberia came into being in 1847, the second oldest independent African nation, the first being Ethiopia.

Alphaeus knew several prominent people in Freetown, who through the years maintained close ties with the Council on African Affairs. He wanted particularly to meet again Mrs. Constance Cummings-Johns, head of the Freetown Society of Young Ladies, who came to the U.S. in the late forties and worked untiringly for two years collecting funds to provide a free school for girls. Alphaeus helped, and on his recommendation, the African Aid Committee made a modest contribution of one hundred dollars. Ten years had passed, and he wondered how the project had thrived.

News of the publication of his book in East Germany, Hungary,

Romania and Bulgaria greeted him on our return. The information brightened the otherwise dull, long haul before summer vacation, except the worker's holiday. Guinea celebrated May first with a colorful, well organized parade that filled the streets for hours with gay, jolly participants, including us.

Fagged out, at the end of our first year, we longed for a change of scenery, diet and some real rest. Alphaeus had lost considerable weight, and his cigarette cough deepened with the passing months, yet he would not cut down or give them up. Malaria had seriously weakened me, along with aches and pains from the dampness. Fortunately, through our friend Danill Semenovich, the Ambassador of the U.S.S.R., the government invited us to the Soviet Union for a complete medical checkup, and we flew to Moscow August, 1951.

After three days with doctors in the Moscow medical clinic, where we underwent examinations to end all examinations, we left with our interpreter, Irena Katagoshchina, for Nizhnaya Oreanda, a famous health sanatorium a few miles from Yalta, on the Black Sea.

Irena, a chaming, vivacious young woman, preparing her thesis on **Nigerian Intelligentsia** at the Africa Institute, beamed with joy at the prospects of plying Alphaeus with questions on Africa, and added much to our stay. No comfort escaped the attendant; flowers, wine, and luscious delicacies always graced our room that looked out on a small, refreshing plot of greenery, somehow cooling the balcony during those very hot days, and there were many.

For three weeks we luxuriated in the cleansing, invigorating air among the tall, stately poplars, and derived much benefit from special diets, relaxing massages, exercises and expert medical attention. The daily rest period in opened rooms down by the sea, listening to the pounding waves against the rugged coastline lulled one to sleep. It brought renewed strength and vigor to our tired bodies, and lifted our drooping spirits. Alphaeus had a serious problem trying to obey doctor's orders: "No cigarettes!" His heart did not function properly, and he chafed miserably under that restraining bit, a severe test of his will; nevertheless, he complied.

One side trip to Sevestopol resulted in a hair-raising experience over high mountains, dangerous curves and narrow roads. The chauffeur's nonchalant enjoyment of fast driving, regardless of the steep climb, frightened us stiff. It took some time and courage before I found my voice long enough to ask him to slow down, much to Alphaeus's displeasure.

Safe at last! We visited the huge Children's Pioneer Camp, viewed the palatial homes of nobleman from the old regime, and marveled at the palace of the last Romanov Czar, Nicholas II where Stalin chose to meet his tough war allies, Franklin D. Roosevelt and Winston Churhill for their historical conference in 1945. The palace now serves as a worker's sanatorium.

Rested and full of energy, we unexpectedly headed south for Tiblisi, capital of Soviet Georgia. Situated in the Caucasus, the crossroads of Asia and Europe, Georgia is linked to distant antiquity with the East, but also blended with European culture. The warm-hearted hospitality of the people and their empathy with Alphaeus and me as Black Americans impressed us. We viewed only a few of the main unique sights of that old city perched high on craggy hills, but we remembered with delight the afternoon spent with a collective farm family. At the request of the cheering men, Alphaeus downed a small ram's horn full of homemade peach brandy, without batting a lash. To refuse would have insulted the host. He seemed none the worse, however, at the end of the day. The mounds of savory food probably turned the tide.

Georgia is noted for its sparkling champagne and smooth cognac. A quick stop at the distillery gave us an idea of the involved process that produced them. Tasting should have come after the visit to Friendship House and the University, as the consciousness of its aroma embarrassed Alphaeus with the African students whose barrage of questions concerning Blacks in the U.S. stretched into a long, animated discussion. He had difficulty breaking away, even after they followed him to the street and continued querying him concerning Africa, the United States and world affairs. The students impressed him by their provocative questions, revealing deep insight, clear thought and a realistic approach to many of the serious problems facing their countries. He regretted time did not permit further debate to clarify some knotty questions. The following morning we left for Central Asia.

A picture of contrast struck us as we entered the modern airport of the 2,000-year-old Tashkent, capital of the Soviet Socialist Republic of Uzbekistan, a city of the old and the new. Once one of the great caravan halting places of Central Asia on the silk route from China to Europe; the fast developing Moslem metropolis lies in the center of a well-watered oasis and is the leading city for transportation in the area. Although the Republic is predominantly Uzbek it consists of many nationalities and one of the main minority groups is Koreans who have lives there a long time, and endured one thing in common with everyone else under the Czar — dehumanizing slavery.

Our petite, bright young girl guide smiled a warm welcome as we deplaned, and escorted us to a new, gleaming, white hotel facing an enormous square. From the balcony, in the cool, desert night, the lights shining on the fontain, in the midst of the square, spouting jets of water twenty to thirty feet in the air that cooled the humid atmosphere in the heat of the day, presented a glistening picture. To bring comfort to the lively pedestrians, we noted that every street and avenue is lined with shady trees fed by irrigation canals.

The new Uzbek Opera House, directly opposite our hotel, was closed for the summer, but the entertainment at suppertime compensated greatly. When the orchestra warmed to the rhythm of a spirited polaka, the gay Uzbeks, who love to dance, filled the small dance space until midnight. After the third Uzbek came to ask Alphaeus's permission to dance with me (a Moslem custom) I finally begged off. To keep up any longer with my partners' fast twirls on the slippery floor would have sealed my doom. Watching me being propelled swiftly over the floor, clinging desperately to my nimble-footed partner, amused Alphaeus. His shyness prevented him from dancing, as much as I pleaded.

Having dealt for years with all kinds of fabrics, the tour through the textile factory fascinated me. The noisy, swift moving looms, hugh vats of dyes and various other operations intrigued Alphaeus as well, considering all the questions he asked. Through our interpreter we spoke to a woman worker who related some dreadful conditions of her mother's life before the Revolution. Deprived of rights by a web of customs, the Moslem society traditionally relegated women strictly to the home. The new wind of social change sweeping through the Moslem countries gives women opportunities to pursue any profession they desire, and many now hold prominent positions in government and industry.

"These mud covered houses look very much like those in Kano," Alphaeus commented as we walked through the narrow, winding streets of Samarkand, the ancient capital of all Central Asia and one of the oldest cities in the world. The feel of centuries long forgotten permeated the city despite the presence of theaters, modern schools and universities. The spirit of old Samarkand still lives. Old men with wispy beards and rawboned bodies sat serenely in the open street cafes, drinking green tea, from small, odd-looking bowls. A plodding monkey with a heavy load, and another, a venerable, old patriarch astride his back, still had right of way in the new market place, piled high with numerous varieties of luscious fruits and vegetables. Samarkand is renowned for the beauty of its fourteenth and fifteenth century architectural treasures. Those unique mosques and palaces, however, were erected by nameless, slave architects. Massive ruins of past glory are still visible in several places, many are being restored brick by brick.

The giant, partially crumbled Bibi-Khanyn Mosque charms many; others, perhaps, take away memories of rectangular Righistan square hemmed in by three mandrassas (colleges). Alphaeus and I admired most the magical street mausoleums, Shadi-Zinda (Living King), that looks like a fairyland on one of Samarkand's slopes, unequaled anywhere in the world. The Gur Emir Tomb of Tamerlane, who by 1404 had subdued half the civilized world, is one of the most striking monuments in Samarkand. Tomb after tomb build over the centuries, each a masterpiece of Oriental architecture with small, glazed tiles and intricate filigree decorating the stately wall are ever-present reminders of the capital's ancient grandeur.

The rushed pace and late hours had little or no effect on our well-being; we returned to Moscow feeling fit and happy. Alphaeus, never at a loss for words appropriate to any occasion, was hard pressed to express his gratitude for the generous help extended us, particularly to Dimitrij Dolidze, Deputy General Secretary of the Soviet Committee for Afro Asian Solidarity. He rounded out the week meeting with officials and giving a lecture on The Question of African Neutralism at the Africa Institute. The topic called forth a barrage of questions. He could have spent the entire afternoon and still not have satisfied the sharp-witted students.

With royalities waiting and invitations extended, Alphaeus arranged to visit Bulgaria, Romania, Hungary and the German Democratic Republic. He had by no means merely a tourist's holiday. Radio and press interviews, a conference at the Academy of Sciences, and a meeting with professors and students at the University kept him exceptionally busy in Budapest. To relieve the day's tension, however, an evening of culture—the opera, ballet or theater served as refreshing breaks.

He especially enjoyed meeting again that venerable humanist and dedicated historian, Dr. Endre Sik, and we shared an evening of stimulating conversation, over excellent Hungarian food, in the cozy Red Star Restaurant while violinists serenaded us with beautiful love songs. Dr. Sik presented Alphaeus with the first volume of his long-awaited **Histoire de l'Afrique Noire,** which was just off the press.

In Bulgaria, life moved at a much slower pace. One incident touched Alphaeus tenderly. After a short stay in Sofia and Plovdiv, we visited a collective farm in Peroushtesta. It boasted a new Hall of Culture, and had a well stocked library. We browsed for awhile, then started down the road to look in on the small tots playing in the village creche. Half way from the hall, we heard someone frantically calling us at the top of her voice. The young librarian, panting and almost out of breath, running down the dusty road, waved a book in her hand — a translation of **Decision in Africa.** Her arms quickly encircled Alphaeus: she kissed him on both cheeks, hugged him tightly, and didn't want to let him go.

The music festival, in full swing when we reached Bucharest, attracted crowds of enthusiasts nightly, and the electrifying symphony concert in the new, ultra-modern, oval concert hall, amply satisfied Alphaeus's strong passion for music. Under the baton of the famous conductor, Sir John Barbirolli, the orchestra moved him almost to tears as they played the compositions of Romania's greatest musician, Georges Enesco.

Here, Alphaeus had no lectures, no interviews, no meetings; merely the enjoyment of genial, Romanian hospitality, and a discussion of his book with the manager of the New Publishing House. The villages we passed on our way to King Carol's Castle in the mountainside seemed poorer than those of Bulgaria. No cultural hall existed, and of course no library, much to Alphaeus' disappointment; but the Castle was replete with marvelous wood carvings and priceless treasures.

A tremendous, colorful poster of an African with the caption, "Give to Support the Schools in Guinea" took us by surprise as we entered the airport in East Berlin. Devastation turned up everywhere, yet the country waged a campaign to assist the African's struggles in the face of mammoth jobs of rebuilding their own land. Our hotel, partly destroyed, had one wing left, and no elevator, but from our window we had an excellent view of West Berlin at night.

Again Alphaeus had an exhaustive schedule from morning to midnight — meetings with officers and members of the German African Society, discussions, speeches, conferences, and radio and press interviews. We visited Stalinstadt, a model industrial city; Dresden, which had been completely destroyed by U.S. bombs in 1945; and Leipzig, where Alphaeus met with the prominent Africanist, Dr. Walter Markov, and with several professors and African students at Karl Marx University.

After two months of absorbing activity and rich rewarding experiences, we settled down in Conakry to prepare for the coming school opening, and to cope with the accumulated mass of green-gray mold on everything from the humidity and dampness. Alphaeus admitted he had planned too extensive an itinerary for such a brief period. His unwillingness to miss a chance to go everywhere and see everything possible provided no more than a short introduction. Regardless of my pleas, no one could stop him, once he got started, and our host in each country gave him an opportunity to observe and learn.

"We may never have such a chance again," he often said. And he had no regrets; only amazement that he had accomplished so much. Though the trip had been hectic, he looked better; gained weight, and felt well, due in the main to good rest and care at Nizhnaya Oreanda.

We plunged into the new semester with renewed zest and determination. Suddenly a new note of expectancy emerged as I listened to Alphaeus read his letter from Dr. Du Bois, in Accra, Ghana, asking him to come work with him in the laborious task of compiling an **Encyclopedia Africana.** Dr. Du Bois, with his wife Shirley, went to Ghana in 1961, at the invitation of President Kwame Nkrumah, for the purpose of launching the **Encyclopedia.** Having worked with Alphaeus in the Council on African Affairs, he wanted his assistance as quickly as possible. At the age of ninety-three, Dr. Du Bois could see that his time was running out.

Years earlier, Dr. Du Bois had conceived the necessity of assembling, in a systematic, encyclopedic form, the entire store of knowledge of African history and culture, analyzed and interpreted from an authentic, African point of view. After two attempts at this great task in the U.S., which had to be abandoned because of lack of financial support, he had found the government of Ghana and its President recognized the value of his efforts and undertook to launch the new project. Alphaeus shared his enthusiasm. Though he found some satisfaction working with the young Guineans, teaching English did not fulfill him. His years of research, and his knowledge of that awakening continent needed a wider scope than the confines of the classroom, and he welcomed the challenge that the Du Bois project offered.

He made a quick visit to Accra to discuss the work, and found Dr. Du Bois none too spry. His decline in health had begun, and he understood the necessity for a speedy beginning, yet his mind retained keenness, as always.

Despite difficult and often trying conditions, working in Guinea had many compensations. We found many things that we thought mattered didn't really matter at all, except to one's vanity. Other things, that we thought didn't matter, carried a great deal of weight. Only three years from under the yoke of the French, who left the country in near ruin, Guinea, with the help of a substantial loan from Ghana, made progress. Plagued by poverty, illiteracy and a desperate shortage of skilled laborers, she survived heavy political, diplomatic and economic pressures to isolate and wreck the new government.

"Some day," Alphaeus wrote several years later, "the Russian-financed technical college may put Conakry on an educational level to equal Dakar and Abidjan as each year it continues to grow."

Yet, he knew obstacles still blocked the path to economic security, and until the Guinean government found ways to exploit her vast natural resources, progress would remain severely limited.

10. GHANA: THE ENCYCLOPEDIA AFRICANA

Coming in by sea to Ghana, after four restful days on a French liner, we watched with strained eyes as the coastline drew nearer, and the slender palm trees, wavering in the haze, emerged. A heat wave greeted us when we arrived in Takoradi, Ghana's only deep-water port, built in 1928, but later extended. The deck of our cargo ship, filled with sightseeing passengers, many leaning on the rails, felt like an oven under the blistering, March sun. This was the hottest time of the year. Ships of many nations packed the harbor, which was in a state of frenzied activity, since the shallow port in Accra made docking impossible. There, seagoing vessels anchored more than a mile offshore waiting for cargo to be paddled to and fro in twenty-four foot surf boats, often bound together in pairs on return trips, to better carry heavy machinery and other bulky goods. Even so, sudden winds and high waves sometimes overturned lighter vessels causing heavy loss of cargo.

For the skilled, muscular crew rowing through the swift surf with freight piled high, jockeying for position among the swaying boats, and bucking the heavy swells, it meant danger. Yet, in late 1961, the government finished one of Africa's largest artificial harbors in Tema, sixteen miles from Accra, that put an end to such hazardous work.

We brought our little red car along, a tiny Czechoslovakian Skoda, far too small for Alphaeus' long legs, but he could get no other in Guinea. He drove with his doubled-up knees projecting above the sides, almost touching his chin. Yet he never complained, for it served him well, though uncomfortably.

Now the stevedores took over and the noisy winches raised higher and higher our precious car, while it dangled in its crib like a dancing puppet. Suspended in mid-air, it stopped — an incredibly long time, Alphaeus thought. I looked at him in apprehension; his eyes met mine, and mine closed. Suddenly the sound of a whistle pierced the air, and the Skoda lurched forward, swinging back and forth. The front wheel leaped over its crib. Surely this was the end, we decided. Finally, it swung over, stopped again, and gently came to rest on the wharf. What a relief! We relaxed, and with our host from the Ghana Academy of Sciences we continued our 130 mile trip to Accra in a government car.

Traffic fairly flew on the hot, tar-paved road to Accra from Takoradi which parallels the shoreline about halfway, then curves inward to avoid the marshes. The long, interesting drive gave Alphaeus and our host an opportunity to discuss that coastal area, and they spoke of the days when Africans were the major export of the Gold Coast. Africans by the thousands had trekked towards the slave pens to be shoved into crowded, dark, airless dungeons in those castle forts we passed. Then they were shipped to the western hemisphere to await the auction block. The antiquated structure of Elmina, the oldest built in 1482, perched high upon a massive rock, dominated the coast line for miles; a grotesque reminder of the hordes of human beings shackled together to meet a fate far worse than death.

Alphaeus wondered aloud from which castle the slaveholders pushed his great grandfather through the watery hole in the dead of night, into a rocking boat below. The sobering thought silenced us awhile; no one seemed able to speak. Only the sound of the Chevrolet's wheels racing over the hot road reached our ears. Alphaeus stared straight ahead, lost in the depth of his reflections.

Windsor Lodge, where we lived for several weeks, faced the green-blue waters of the Gulf of Guinea. It stood just a few yards from the Danish fortress, Christianburg Castle, Osu, situated on a steep, rocky cliff hanging out over the sea. The spot is beautiful, quiet, but with an eerie silence, broken in the early dawn by the ever-crowing rooster and the sound of waves crashing against the rocks as if to drown the cries of those hapless creatures whose moans still reverberate through the damp, castle walls. Christianburg now serves as Government House. Yet, the aroma of blood, sweat and breath, does not escape the nostrils of a sensitive soul, despite the fragrant flowers in the castle's well-kept garden.

The entire area suddenly comes alive weekends, especially on Sundays, when young people and families with romping children take over the sandy beach. Those weekends Alphaeus loved. Sitting among the good natured Ghanaians, he came to appreciate their hearty enjoyment of life while listening to their zestful laughter and the men's excited palaver. A bit of their gaiety rubbed off on him, but not for long, as he instinctively hid his true feelings from the world. His soft voice and disarming smile never failed to attract, especially women, who admired his careless grace and natural elegance.

Alphaeus appreciated this extra time to recharge his energies. He welcomed the cool breeze while waiting for a house and for Dr. Du Bois' return form Europe, where he was undergoing treatment. The work ahead would be grueling, requiring all the mental and physical strength he could muster. Just the thought of being relieved from wrestling daily with French, and correcting endless stacks of papers, sufficed for my keenest pleasure. Yet, Alphaeus soon became restless, as he usually did when time dragged and nothing specific occupied his days. He longed to get on with the job.

We finally settled in a spacious, cozy bungalow with a screened veranda on three sides, that permitted evening enjoyment free from the perpetual menace of flies and mosquitoes. It was far from the sea, however, but cool, in a high, wooded section once reserved exclusively for British officers and high officials and barred to all Africans not carrying special passes as servants.

The debilitating effects of the West Coast climate and the infestation of the deadly mosquitoes (carrying one of Africa's most devastating diseases, malaria) kept large numbers of Europeans from settling here as they did in Zambia, East Africa and Southern Rhodesia where the temperature is more endurable. Hence, winning independence in Ghana was less complicated. In other African territories the pressure of a large and dominant European population, determined to hold on to their possessions and privileges, put up stiff resistance.

Soon after our arrival, Alphaeus expressed in a letter to President Nkrumah his joy at the opportunity to come back to Ghana. This time, he hoped it would be for good. He welcomed the privilege of being associated, however indirectly and insignificantly, with the administration, and indicated his astonishment at the national development, both material and ideological, that had taken place since his first visit in December 1958, on the occasion of the All African People's Conference.

"The ideological advance is...especially remarkable and trustworthy," he wrote, "and is at the same time the essential factor accounting for the great material accomplishments. For this, as well as for your remarkable contribution to the cause of world peace, I pay homage to your wise and able leadership."

The President greeted us warmly on our first visit to his office. He and Alphaeus embraced heartily, like long-lost brothers, and reminisced over Nkrumah's hectic years in the United States. A shrewd politican and diplomat, he radiated genial charm, and I noticed that his eyes never left you during a conversation.

Alphaeus and Nkrumah had met many years earlier in connection with Council on African Affairs activities. They vividly recalled the conference, organized in 1944, to project an international program for postwar liberation of Africa. Kwame Nkrumah, a serious and articulate young student, took an active part. A leader in the West African Student Union, he studied at Lincoln University and the University of Pennsylvania. Already an avowed nationalist, he bent all his efforts toward seeking autonomy for the Gold Coast. After taking further studies at the London School of Economics and law at University College in England, he returned home, intensified his efforts towards his objective, and became the principal spokesman for unity among independent African states.

A new era began for Africans when Nkrumah became Prime Minister after a long and bitter campaign of civil disobedience in which he was twice jailed. Alphaeus, over the years, had never failed to follow his stony path. We applauded him along with thousands of others when he visited Conakry in 1960, and again in 1961 when we heard him speak at the Kremlin, following his Soviet tour. To Alphaeus, Nkrumah symbolized a brilliant, scintillating light penetrating centuries of darkness. It was a call to Blacks in America, and to people of African descent everywhere to show pride in their African heritage.

The bungalow assigned the Encyclopedia Secretariat shaped up well, with a few innovations from Alphaeus. At home, too, he lost no time building bookshelves and other equipment for his study. Ghana's tropical forests teem with some of the world's finest hardwoods. Mahogany and other high quality timber, which cost a fortune on the European market, are so common that roadside carpenters use them for the most unessential items.

From the feel of Alphaeus's soft hands one would think he never did any hard labor work. But they were huge, and his thick wrists made it easy for him to manipulate the electric saw. In our basement in New York he made a number of articles for his study, including his desk.

With everything in order, he immersed himself in the formidable task of drawing up a preliminary draft of plans for the contents and organization of the proposed **Encyclopedia Africana.** Dr. Du Bois had corresponded with a large number of scholars in and outside of Africa and had received "affirmation of the need and feasibility of such an undertaking." He saw the work "as entailing the maximum cooperation among African scholars and institutions representing thus another path toward Pan-African Unity. It would provide a definitive answer to all racist myths and lies, and be one of inestimable value to Africans and those of African descent in this period of revolutionary change and intellectual renaissance."

The Secretariat intended to draw also upon writings of non-African specialists in the various disciplines whose works had contributed to the accurate interpretation of African life and history. Cooperation of such scholars in all parts of the world was eagerly sought. While the center of direction an co-ordination remained in Accra, the Secretariat invited all Africa to participate in the work.

In June, after four months' work, Alphaeus issued the first eight-page monthly information bulletin, **For Cooperation Toward an Encyclopedia Africana.** Later a twenty-four page document defined the scope, size, organization and main contents of the proposed Encyclopedia, which was to be published in French, English and Arabic. Copied were sent to members of an Advisory Committee composed of leading figures in the Institute of African Studies at the University of Ghana, Legon, headed by Professor J.H. Nketia. With their cooperation, the provisional draft was ready for consideration by December 18, 1962.

More then one hundred and fifty participants, representing a wide geographical distribution, took part in the conference on the proposal. The articles were often hotly debated, and it took some ingenuity to smooth a few ruffled feathers, but the enthusiasm shown by the delegates left no doubt in anyone's mind of the need for the **Encyclopedia Africana.** At the opening session, Dr. Du Bois gave his last speech before his death in his capacity as director of the organization and said:

> It is true scientific written records do not exist in most parts of the vast continent, but the time is now for the beginning. The Encyclopedia hopes to eliminate the artificial boundaries created on the continent by colonial masters. Designations such as "British Africa," "French Africa," "Black Africa," "Islamic Africa," too often serve to keep alive differences which in large part have been imposed on Africans by outsiders...We are deeply grateful to the President of Ghana and to the Government of this independent state for inviting us to undertake this important task here where the necessary funds for beginning this colossal work have been provided. After all, this is where the work should be done--in Africa, sponsored by Africans, for Africa. This Encyclopedia will be carried through.

In order to coordinate the work, the delegates agreed that the Encyclopedia should have research units in North, East, South, West and Central Africa, to gather information for those geographical sections. The huge area could not be covered by a single central committee. It required feeding committees contributing to the central body of the Board of Editors. Alphaeus began establishing communications with scholars in the five regions.

The pressure and strain of trying to lay the foundation of the Encyclopedia exhausted Alphaeus to such an extent that we took a two week rest on a French freighter down the coast to Pointe Noire, Brazzaville

Congo. The brief stopover at six ports afforded a welcomed break and gave him an opportunity to renew old acquaintances and meet new friends.

The trial of the suspected bomb throwers, who had tried to kill Nkrumah before we left, reached its heights when we returned. A previous attempt on his life had killed several bystanders, and the people were up in arms. Since Nkrumah formed the Convention People's Party (C.P.P.) in 1949, based on the support of the broad masses, including youth, after he found it impossible to work with the slow-moving, conservative United Gold Coast Convention organization as general secretary, the opposition against him never ceased. "The leaders never forgave me," he said. "They became implacable opponents of the Party, determined to obstruct its progress at every stage, and to attack me personally on all possible occasions."[2]

Ghana, unlike Guinea, had retained the institution of Chiefs, and Nkrumah tried to merge traditional tribalism with the modern science of government by going into the countryside and meeting directly with the largely illiterate villagers. One important characteristic of chieftancy is the preservation of the cultural heritage. Although living through a time of fundamental change and feverish construction, Ghanaians did not forget their ancient past. Neither did internal subversion and outside interference prevent the government from pursuing its appointed goal.

The need to diversify the economy, which depended heavily on the African-owned cocoa farms, the world's greatest producers, grew desperate as prices fluctuated. Yet, education received the greatest push. Knowledge was the prime need of the hour, and education became compulsory. Nkrumah knew the country could make no better investment than providing adequate schooling for the masses, and he introduced free education from primary to university level.

The number of schools and colleges built in the five years of independence — the pride of Ghana and an example to the entire continent, amazed Alphaeus. He recalled the untiring efforts of another farsighted, beloved Ghanaian, Dr. J.E.K. Aggrey.

Dr. Aggrey was one of the founders of Achimota College, situated on a magnificent site, then an uncultivated hill covered with grass, eight miles from Accra. It was a place of ill omen; Achimota meant, "Do not mention the name." But when the school opened in 1927, the word acquired a new significance. [3]

Though Dr. Aggrey had lived in the U.S. for twenty years, he, more than anyone else, contributed to establishing the great reputation for the school and college, which created a boon to Africans eager for education. As it expanded to a University College, it became the educational center of British West Africa. "Only the best is good enough for

Africa," Aggrey said. "I want all my people, my countrymen, women and children, to be educated in the larger sense, in the heart, hand and head, and thus render Africa indispensable in spiritual, intellectual and commercial products to the world."

Few African capitals remain quiet places, and Accra, one of the most active cities along the coast, least of all. The bustling, rapidly growing metropolis had an unique, cosmopolitan atmosphere despite its sea of tin-roofed houses amid new high-rising structures. A stimulating liveliness permeated the air. One felt this especially at the small, experimental theatre where Africans staged their own plays in unusual and traditional African settings. One could see much artistic skill in their improvising with the scarce props available. The theatre always held a warm attraction for Alphaeus, and he never missed a play.

Of equal enjoyment were those rare, musical evenings that he referred to as "old home week." All our friends were there. Europeans and Ghanaians had formed an orchestra, and their excellent performances drew record crowds. Unlike Americans, however, African audiences are rather restrained in their reaction; their applause more often than not subdued and polite, never resounding. Yet, that does not mean they are not as deeply moved.

The vividness and intensity of the Ghanaian culture truly comes alive during the celebration of traditional festivals. Once a year, old and young share the activities, and women dancers take the lead in stimulating the crowd. We witnessed one spring festival that was full of dignity and richness of centuries. Yet, it seemed mild compared to that most colorful pageantry a **durba** — a gathering of sub-chiefs and their followers to greet the paramount chief, or a very special occasion.

The Paramount Chief, who speaks only to lesser people through his linguist, rides in a palanquin attended by his retinue. An immense, brilliantly colored ceremonial umbrella that bounces and sways shades him from the sun while the followers mill around the field. Giant drums pounded by quick, strong hands give forth astonishing sounds. Coupled with the shrill calls of the women, and the shattering blast of the trumpets, the excitement makes one's scalp prickle. The chiefs, in all their ancient splendor, wear of course, the famous Kente cloth that dates back 250 years. Extremely expensive, the beautiful multicolored silk and cotton strips are delicately designed and hand-woven on narrow, simple looms, then sewn together. Most are interwoven with soft, yellow gold, that precious metal the Portuguese repeatedly exploited from the Gold Coast chiefs long before Columbus discovered America.

Small boys begin to practice on miniature looms at an early age as the art is handed down from father to son. Each pattern represents a clan or proverb, and each has its own name.

Black Americans did not walk alone when thousands marched to Washington on August 28, 1963, to bring home to the U.S. government that the time had come to give equality of citizenship to Blacks. In Accra, more than 200 Black Americans and supporters organized a demonstration of solidarity with the historic march. With placards that told the woeful story of indignities suffered in their own country, the demonstrators, led by Alphaeus, picketed the U.S. Embassy. After an all-night vigil, they marched through the principal streets of the city and later, with a delegation of five, presented a petition to Mr. Oliver L. Troxel, the acting chief of the mission of the U.S. Embassy, for transmission to President Kennedy.

The petition called on the President to grant and guarantee constitutional rights to Black citizens in the U.S. "We remind you," it said, "that 20 million Americans of African descent are products of more than 300 years of American slavery and inferior status in a white supremacist society, which boasts to the world that it is the land of the free and the home of the brave. Such a boast is hollow as long as America's Black citizens are denied the fundamental liberties which white citizens take for granted."

While the demonstrators walked back and forth in the warm, sultry night, holding their placards high, the man who grappled all his life with affairs of humanity, bringing clarity where confusion hid, and courage where faintheartedness once prevailed, lay upon his bed waiting patiently for that well deserved rest that would release him from a tired body. Peacefully, Dr. Du Bois' spirit slipped away.

Knowing that the end was near, I did not join Alphaeus in the demonstration, but stayed through the night with his wife Shirley Du Bois. Dr. Sarah Lee, Lt. Christian Debrah (sent by Nkrumah) and I, tried to give some help and comfort during that solemn evening. Dr. Du Bois had lived to see at least the practical beginning of one of his lifelong ambitions, the **Encyclopedia Africana.**

I once accompanied Dr. Du Bois on one of his daily, afternoon auto rides along the palm-lined shore between Accra and Tema. Dr. Du Bois disliked riding alone. The route always the same, brought into view the Fanti fishing crews in their carved, gaily painted canoes, hollowed from a single tree trunk. Other fishermen swam in the powerful surf, trying desperately to close their nets. On shore, the rhythmic chanters sang louder and louder with each pull of the heavy net, and finally hauled in the bulging mesh squirming with the long day's catch. The women, always gay in their bright, colorful prints, laughed and chatted balancing their empty baskets on their heads while waiting for the headman to supervise the division of the fish.

All was peaceful and serene as we drove on until suddenly on the horizon, a jolting "Mammy Truck" loomed high. Knowing no speed limit, and recognizing no curves, it came tearing down the narrow road as if no one else was visible. The driver's favorite sign painted on the rumbling vehicle in huge, glaring letters, **Remember Thy Creator in the Days of Thy Youth** did not placate our young driver who swerved over just in time as it whizzed by in a cloud of dust, baggage rattling and the occupants holding on to their seats for dear life.

These conveyances are ordinary light pickup trucks fitted with planked seats, some equipped with props to hold up awnings that keep out the blazing sun. But all are packed solid with passengers and baggage. Though a great hazard to safety, they nevertheless meet a specific need as the only means of transportation for those in the hinterland. Rarely did I see one of those rigged up jungle beasts zooming down the road without a motto. **All Shall Pass** read one. Yet he lets no one pass, if he can help it. A young man hurriedly took to the ditch when one bounced by him displaying the phrase **Life Is War.**

The flavor is purely Ghanaian, and gives cause for reflection to **The Life—What Have you Done!** But it consoles no one on the highway who meets the vehicle, hogging the middle of the road honking frantically while the sign **Who Knows the End** hanging in front shakes violently, and **Fear Not: Death Comes Suddenly,** brings up the rear.

In late September, Alphaeus spoke at the College of Technology, Science and Art at Kumasi, on the **Encyclopedia Africana.** It was my first visit to that historic province, once the heart of one of West Africa's most important civilizations, the Ashantis. For centuries past, they measured gold dust by balancing it on scales against counterweights of inferior metals, usually bronze or brass. Beautifully wrought in forms of birds, fish and other creatures, those counterweights are now valued museum pieces.

Heading north from Accra in our small Skoda, I thought for a moment Alphaeus intended to compete with the "Mammy Truck" that sped past us with its thoughtful sign, **Don't Worry, God's Time Is Best.** As slow and deliberate as he usually acted in the regular routine of life, the wide-open road never failed to release the brakes that normally held him in check, and away he went, enjoying every minute of it. Uninterested in the scenery, he looked straight ahead.

Sections of the road become dangerous as you dip and climb through the wooded area. I tried to refrain from acting like a backseat driver. But as we hit that spot on our return, I repeated my warning to slow down — unfortunately to closed ears. Suddenly there was a sharp turn Alphaeus had not anticipated. He struggled desperately to control the car, but in vain. His words, "This is it," stunned me as the car sped down the hill and left the road, turning over three times on its way. It finally came to a stop, upright in a field, miles from nowhere.

With the back seat resting heavily on my back, and broken glass all around, I couldn't move. Alphaeus's arm, badly cut, and bleeding profusely, hung out the window. His fingers, completely covered with blood and dirt, were scarcely visible.

"Are you all right dear?" he asked, almost in a whisper.

I was too shocked and angry to answer. Somehow he freed himself and dragged me out, and sheepishly asked my forgiveness.

Fortunately, a doctor passed by and gave us first aid, but a crutial problem remained - where to find a clinic? For more than an hour we trudged around, and eventually came to a small clinic, deep in the interior, but no doctor was available; only an assistant.

"I can sew your arm up," the assistant said, "but I have only aspirins to deaden the pain."

The agony that gripped Alphaeus reflected in his tense expression, still he did not complain as he watched the nurse assemble her surgical instruments.

"Don't worry, it won't take long," the assistant said, as he carefully cleaned the arm and gave it another quizzical look.

Alphaeus braced himself and bore up well. But when I saw his eyes become moist as he fought to hold back the tears from excruciating pain, I couldn't bear to watch and left the room. The surgery completed, we went in search of someone to tow us to Accra.

The car would have been stripped of everything usable had we left it overnight, and Alphaeus was determined to get it home. We arrived in Accra near midnight. Trying to steer the car with one hand, while it banged against the truck every other foot added to his woes. That horrendous night he never forgot. Exhausted, and in misery as he prepared for bed, he said again contritely, "Forgive me dear, I'm sorry." Never again did he call me a backseat driver.

In March 1963, the reconstituted Ghana Academy of Sciences, of which Kwame Nkrumah was President, had informed the **Encyclopedia Africana Secretariat** that it had been formally incorporated into the Council. This had disturbed Dr. Du Bois and Alphaeus; they had received the understanding from the President that the Academy would assist, advise and cooperate with the Secretariat, but would not undertake to direct or control its affairs. While the work had been initiated in Ghana, it was not to be a Ghanaian product by any means. As the project developed, it would naturally involve scholars, institutions and financial contributors, they hoped, from other independent African states. Their concern was solely preserving the independent chacter of the Secretariat as far as possible, and that new development had called for critical analysis and frank understanding.

Any general Pan-African participation in the work would surely prejudice its efforts if it appeared that any one state, or its agencies, sought to maintain exclusive or dominant control. Disagreement arose over differences in views as to the qualifications and duties of persons Alphaeus needed on the staff, and he had the impression that the Academy did not appreciate the idea that the Secretariat was a free body, making its own decisions.

Early in September 1963, a Working Committee for the Secretariat was established for the purpose of assuming responsibility for some of the duties exercised by the late Director. The Committee chairman was William E. Abraham, Professor of Philosophy at the University of Ghana, and M.F. Dei-Anang, of the African Affairs Secretariat, Office of the President, in association with two members of the Secretariat staff, Alphaeus, as Secretary, and Lebrecht W. Hessee, Research Officer.

With the cooperation of the Academy of Sciences and the courtesy of scholars in North and East Africa, Alphaeus arranged a tour to promote the operation of Regional Committees in those areas, and in November 1963 he flew to Cairo. (I had left in October to visit my family in New York, on one of Ghana's new ships, Afram River, a freighter and a product of the country's proud Black Star Shipping Line, jointly formed with Israel.)

The leader of the Regional Committee, Dr. Abdel-Malik Auda, Professor of Political Science at Cairo University, met Alphaeus at the airport, welcomed him with a "European embrace," and took him to the Nile Hilton Hotel, as a guest of the government. For two days he met with officials and university people. He addressed two meetings arranged for members of the Egyptian Geographical Society, the Egyptian Scientific Union, an organization embracing several research institutions concerned with natural and applied sciences, and the Egyptian Society for Legislation, Economics and Statistics.

Some of the members expressed considerable concern that Egypt should have a significant part in the work. They wanted to know who controlled the project, how the Secretariat proposed to acquire money and staff. Their questions touched on the very points Alphaeus had hammered away at for months with the Academy of Sciences, in his attempt to show that the project could not be exclusively a Ghanaian affair.

After four days of constant activity, a weekend excursion to view the ancient monuments at Luxor provided some relaxation. Cairo, teeming with people, cars and buses fascinated Alphaeus. But more meetings and interviews filled his remaining days, and left no time for sightseeing.

"It's been an extremely busy day," Alphaeus wrote, "I think I've talked with almost every important person in official and intellectual circles except Nasser himself." The government and university people assured their support, and Alphaeus was gratified by their enthusiasm. "They're expecting big things of us in Accra," he continued, " and we cannot afford to fail."

Just before the farewell dinner given by the Minister of Higher Education, Alphaeus held a hurriedly arranged meeting with twenty or thirty African students studying in Cairo at the hostel provided for foreign students. Their eagerness to help stirred him tremendously, and he found the gathering a fitting finale to an encouraging beginning.

As promising as the talks were in Cairo, there was less enthusiasm for the project in Khartoum, capital of the Sudan, and once a bustling slave mart. One stimulating group discussion occurred with Dr. Ibrahim Hassan, of the Department of Geography, University of Khartoum presiding, and individual talks with the Vice-Chancellor of the University, Dr.Al-Nazar Dafaals; Professor Abdulla El-Tayib, Dean of the Faculty of Arts; Professor Mekki Shibeika, Head of the Department of History; Dr. G. N. Sanderson, Director of the Sudan Research Unit then in process of organization at the University; Thabit Hassan Thabit, National Commissioner for Archaeology, and Sayed Ibrahim Nur, Permanent Under-Secretary of the Ministry of Education.

As the guest of the University, Alphaeus stayed in a hotel just opened a week previous. Though not quite as elegant as the Nile Hilton, it was modern and comfortable, but it had one drawback. "The bathroom door was six inches too low," he complained, "and I got plenty of bumps on my head before I learned to duck."

In quiet, leisurely Khartoum, he felt none of the metropolitan air of Cairo. Some sections reminded him of Conakry, though Khartoum is ten times as large. Africans live mostly in Omdurman, a busy, mud-brick city across the river, and there is a lot of taxiing to and fro, just like in Donka. They also use the same system — everybody crowding in and sharing the fare.

True to form, his yen to see all he could of any country caused his host to arrange a trip in a Volkswagen bus to some old, Egyptian-built temples about 125 miles from Khartoum. He really saw what the Sudan is like. No roads existed except automobile tracks through sandy and scrubland wastes, with only here and there some nomadic shepherds and a few small scattered villages of rectangular mud huts common to all Moslem countries. It was the roughest, dirtiest automobile ride he had ever taken, and a couple of times they almost got stuck in the sand. Nature provides the Sudan with little more than the means for meager living. "I thought we'd never get back to Khartoum," he said, "and the professor in charge of me [who didn't go along] had expected us back earlier, and got so nervous he sent out a police alarm for us." Fortunately, they had an expert driver and arrived safely.

In Addis Ababa, Dr. Richard Pankhurst, Director of the Institute of Ethiopian Studies, organized a meeting with a number of important people interested in the Encyclopedia. Alphaeus had discussions with members of the U.N. Economic Commission, and also met with other gatherings where he gave less formal presentations of the plans.

To many, Ethiopia seemed the ageless, remote Tibet of Africa; an undisturbed, mysterious country just beginning to realize, after centuries of isolation, that an incomparable world existed beyond her towering mountains. Alphaeus had no time to take any excursions into the interior, but he did manage one all day motor trip by land rover to a mountain, some fifty miles away. He found it "rough going up the mountains, but not near as troublesome and tiring, and far more interesting than the motor trip in the Sudan."

Ethiopia's scenic beauty, the fresh, cool climate, even the cold, brisk nights refreshed him. The villages, cupped in the sheltering, green hills, backed by rugged mountains, and the profusion of beautiful flowers, and lush vegetation everywhere, brought an exhilarating change from the dry, hot, barren Sudan environment. But the sight of the ragged poor in their abject misery, and the hobbling, dreadfully deformed beggars disturbed him, as did the high altitude his first day while walking through the hilly streets.

At the end of his five day tour, the Sudanese Ambassador, Dr. Jamal Mohammed Ahmed, gave a reception for Alphaeus, much to his surprise, with the Ghana Ambassador present. The results in Addis Ababa, in terms of his mission, proved positive.

Nairobi's modern, big-city character with its good, clean streets, sidewalks, and up-to-date stores surprised Alphaeus. Yet he knew quite well that the thatched African villages on the outskirts presented a vastly different picture. Memories of the bloody Mau-Mau days in the nineteen fifties flooded his mind. In **Spotlight on Africa,** he had exposed the real cause of the festering sore that spread over the entire body of the colony. Now, in a few days, December 12, Kenya would be free.

The white settlers and wealthy Indians through the years had built up many enterprises, thinking they would live there forever. Yet, with coming independence, some just couldn't take it, and thousands left in droves, while others resigned themselves to African rule — or said they did. Indians still owned practically all the property in the city, and the British owned most of the fertile farmland. Nevertheless, the African government had already started doing away with the long-standing separation of Europeans, Asians and Africans in every phase of life by ordering the integration of schools. "Rather than admit Kenyans," Alphaeus said, "one white school closed down, just like our southern U.S.A."

Independence and festivities made it difficult for him to make appointments, but numerous chance encounters with visitors with whom he had corresponded compensated for that loss. Talks with some members of the faculty of the University College of Uganda especially pleased him, as Kampala, unfortunately, was not on his itinerary. He also managed to have discussions with Mr. K.S.N. Matiba, Permanent Secretary in the Ministery of Education, Dr. Gikonyo Kiano, Minister of Commerce and Industry, and Dr. J.N. Karanja, then lecturer in history at Royal College, who, three days after their talk, was appointed High Commissioner for Kenya in London. A hastily arranged gathering took place in a hotel lounge on Alphaeus' last day, that resulted in one of his most stimulating so far.

He had completed a month's traveling and accepted an invitation to the independence celebration in Tanzania. Sweltering Dar es Salaam's heat, he thought of Accra's sultriness — but Dar struck him as being much worse. He was welcomed at the home of Dr. Terence O. Ranger, Professor of history at the new university, situated on a hill overlooking the surrounding country with the Indian Ocean in the distance.

Dr. Ranger, an Englishman, whom the Southern Rhodesian government had recently expelled for his association with the Nationalist Movement, presided over a meeting of a few people keenly interested in the Encyclopedia. Though a small group, the animated discussions and optimism of the professors did much to encourage Alphaeus. At the end of his two day visit, he attended the freedom celebrations in Zanzibar, which he thought "splendid but rather restrained emotionally."

Kenya's Independence Celebration was far from restrained. "It was the most tremendous spectacle I've ever seen," he wrote. "Imagine an area as big as Yankee Stadium with about twenty-five groups of different tribal dancers and musicians — 1200 in all — moving around and all performing simultaneously." He had never witnessed such dancing.

Thousands flocked into Nairobi. Some in tribal dress, some in patched and tattered, but clean western clothes, some bare-footed. But all carried a flag or wore a pin for **UHURU** (freedom).

When the East African tour finished, Alphaeus was glad to take off for Belgrade, for his mind felt heavy and soggy. In Belgrade he was busy going from one institute to another, then having dinner with the former Ambassador in Accra, Mr. Zvonko Perisic, whose farewell reception in September we failed to attend. He had time for only a quick look at a few beauty spots in the snow clad city before departure for Hungary.

In a very high-ceilinged room with big, plush chairs neatly placed in a circle, Alphaeus met his hosts in the Establishment of the Hungarian Academy of Sciences. He had two meetings, which his friend Dr. Sik attended. Since that portion of his three month trip was, at least, supposed to be part vacation, he tried to keep his engagements down to a minimum, and get some rest. Yet, the usual rounds of newspaper and radio interviews could not be denied, nor talks with professionals interested in Africa.

No one told Alphaeus that the restaurants and theatres closed on Christmas Eve. Streets became empty after 5 P.M. Celebrations took place in the home. He had nowhere to go and nothing to do, and felt completely outside of the holiday merriment — a sad and lonely Christmas Eve. At nine o'clock, he went to bed, without even a radio for companionship.

Christmas day turned out better, when his guide and interpreter came and made plans to brighten his stay. Except for two short trips outside the city, he took it fairly easy. A three day jaunt at the Trade Union resort, he especially enjoyed, despite the uncomfortable bed, which, as usual, never fitted his size. The New Year's festivities however, made up for all the physical discomforts of sleeping. "There was a special party for the guest," he wrote, "and you probably won't believe me, but I **did** dance a couple of dances." With ping-pong, which he loved, indoor swimming and other activities, he had plenty to relax his mind as well as his body. The brisk morning walks in the cold air refreshed him while he watched the skiers make dangerous jumps amidst the frosty landscape. It made him long to extend the visit further.

Another attempt was made on Nkrumah's life on January 1, 1964, in the garden of Flagstaff House as he left his office on his way to lunch. The would-be assassin, a policeman on guard, fired four shots, all ineffective. A fifth shot killed a loyal security officer who had spotted him among the trees and ran towards him. The policeman then tried to hit Nkrumah with his rifle. Nkrumah managed to overpower him until help arrived, but not before he had bitten him on the cheek. [5]

News of the incident distressed Alphaeus severely, and he weighed the question of returning to Accra, though he had no idea what role he could play, if any. The assignment in North Africa still remained unfinished, and he didn't relish the idea of cancelling it on his own initiative. When he wired Flagstaff House and received no reply, he stopped in Prague two days with the George Wheelers, then moved on to Geneva, where the Ghanaian Ambassador assured him the situation continued calm, and he saw no need to change his plans. Alphaeus left immediately for North Africa.

At each destination, a representative of the Ghana Embassy met him. In Algiers he would have had a rough time had that precaution not been taken. Despite letters and arrangements made in Accra, no one seemed to know of his coming, and that upset Alphaeus's usual calmness. While he recognized the difficulties in bringing together a group on the spur of the moment, he had moderate success finding a few concerned people to talk with individually. Actually, he spent only two days in

Algiers, but he thought it wise to make the stop-over, however brief. He judged every effort indispensable, if it encouraged just one more person to take a stand in promoting the project.

In Tunis, where the University served as host, the tempo accelerated far beyond his expectations. He accomplished a great deal, due primarily to a well organized group under an energetic young leader, Professor A. Bouhdiba, of the Centre d'Etudes et de Recherches Economiques et Sociales. Professor Bouhdiba arranged a program that allowed no wasted time, and every minute Alphaeus spent profitably. It buoyed him up considerably after the unexpected let-down in Algiers.

Alphaeus found little in Tunis to attract his attention, and it appeared to him rather drab. Algiers, on the otner hand, "is one of the most beautiful cities I've seen," he said, "and very much alive."

In Rabat, he stayed with our friend of long standing, Mario de Andradra, a fervent enthusiast of the Encyclopedia, and a dedicated advocate of African freedom, especiaily for his country, Angola, still in the throes of Portuguese domination. Though less organized, and small in numbers, those who gathered to discuss the work showed warmth and earnestness. That, too, fortified him, and gave him hope on the last stage of his African mission.

The short visits accomplished more in advancing the organization and work of the cooperating units than could have been achieved through long months of correspondence. Alphaeus's diplomatic nature, his gift of getting to the core of a matter, and his appreciation of different points of view stimulated and inspired fresh interest in the Encyclopedia project. And his unwearied patience stirred those already involved to transform their good intentions into substantial action.

"Most important, perhaps," he commented on his return, "the tour confirmed and gave concrete demonstration of the fact that the Secretariat in Accra, and its sponsors, see Pan-African cooperation on the **Encyclopedia Africana** project as not only desirable but absolutely essential."

Picketing U.S. Embassy, Accra, Ghana, August 1963

Chinese officials, Academy of Science, Peking, China, 1965

Dinner given by the Academy of Sciences, Peking, China, 1965

Indonesian Ambassador and wife, Indonesian Embassy
Accra, Ghana, 1965

*Julian Mayfiend, Maya Angelou, Dr. Wendell Jean-Pierre, Sr., Alphaeus,
Inside U.S. Embassy, Accra, Ghana, presenting a petition to President Kennedy
August 1963*

*Chinese officials, Ambassador Huang Hau next to Alphaeus
Accra, Ghana, 1965*

Alphaeus, Dr. Sarah Lee, Dorothy
Mali reception, Accra, Ghana, 1965

11. SHATTERED HOPES: THE GHANAIAN COUP

Alphaeus felt relieved to be back in Ghana, but bemoaned the fact that he greeted an empty house. Twice my departure on the Black Star Liner had been postponed. Instead of leaving New York as scheduled, passengers had to embark in New Orleans, Louisiana, where again there was a week's delay.

I knew no one in New Orleans, and arrived at midnight. A redcap promptly steered me to a Y.W.C.A., which had been desegregated just a week before. Another stroke of good luck broke the frustrating layover. The fabulous Mardi Gras started the following day, and took the edge off my annoyance.

At last we sailed, but the trip was far from restful. In mid-ocean a frightening disturbance arose between the African crew and the white officers, and we remained in Dakar, Senegal, for four days. The engineers refused to work until an official from Ghana arrived to settle the dispute. The month-long crossing finally ended, and I welcomed the blistering sun in humid Accra, but most of all Alphaeus's warm and tender embrace.

Knowing his difficulties in revealing pure affection, especially in view of anyone, I watched how quickly his countenance changed as his old reserve crumbled and a big, broad smile transformed his face. His eyes bespoke the rising tide of emotion that his voice was unable to utter, despite elaborate casualness to keep it in check. But I understood. It was one of those rare moments to remember, moments of unspoken love that gave comfort and assurance with wonderful dependability over the years.

The March rains, which would soon become a downpour, overflowing the culverts and changing some dirt roads into a mass of mud, made me impatient to plant my new seeds. Gardening had grown into a rewarding hobby since my decision to engage in but one job — the world's most diversified and demanding, housewife. The acute shortage of green vegetables (not basic in the Ghanaian diet), made it mandatory to take advantage of the large, unused area surrounding our house.

With my unquenchable optimism, I set out to conquer the hordes of insects without the dreaded D.D.T. The first years' organic experiment of trial and error not only gave moderate success and confidence, but a deeper appreciation of the humble farmer who struggles constantly with soil factors and climatic vagaries. There was no lack of encouragement on Alphaeus's part; he enjoyed the fruits of my labor and took pride in my achievement.

Alphaeus continued to intensify his efforts towards developing a continental network of Cooperating Committees functioning in close liaison with the coordinating center in Accra. He corresponded with leaders or prospective leaders of such committees in thirty-eight African countries. Those committees selected members for the Editorial Board. The appointment of the Editorial Board and its staff, however, raised the question of all-African responsibility for the work of the Secretariat. The Working Committee agreed that while financial grants might be obtained from U.N. Agencies, like U.N.E.S.C.O., it would be more appropriate to associate African governments under the Organization of African Unity with the Encyclopedia work. Consequently, the O.A.U. Heads of States endorsed the resolution at their meeting in Accra, in 1965, calling upon member states to give all possible support to the project.

At the first meeting of the Editorial Board, in September 1964, at the University of Ghana, thirty-one members or alternates, representing twenty-two of the twenty-nine countries that had agreed to serve on the Board attended.

Dr. Kwama Nkrumah, in his opening speech, said, "It was yet another token of the African cultural renaissance which is manifesting itself side by side with the political resurgence of the African continent." While expressing his appreciation of the "world-wide support of the idea of an Encyclopedia Africana" as indicated by endorsements received by the Secretariat, the President noted that "it is only logical that an encyclopedic work on Africa should be produced in Africa, under the direction and editorship of Africans, and with the maximum participation of African scholars in all countries."

He expressed the hope that the work would "provide both the forum and the motivation for the development of a virile and salutary new trend in writing African history, writing which will rank in scholarship with any other historiography, but which will also be based upon a frame of reference that is independently African, and will lead the way in independent thinking about Africa and its problems."

It was estimated that the **Encyclopedia Africana** would contain approximately ten million words, and consist of ten volumes. Nearly half of the first volume would be devoted to materials designed to give the reader a general understanding of the sources and broad chronology of African history and a summary of the main contents of all the other volumes.

Volume II would consist solely of articles on each of the present-day African states, together with surrounding islands that are individually administered. Volume III would consist entirely of biographies. Volume IV-X would include Arts and Literature, Economy and Resources, Education, Ethnic Groups and Languages, Health, History to 1900, History since 1900, Traditional Social Institutions, Laws and Customs.

In addition to those materials, representing the main content of Volumes IV-X, there would be several thousand short articles relating to non-edible plants that are characteristic of or peculiar to the African landscape; birds, reptiles and other animals normally found only in various regions of Africa; geographical place-names, such as rivers, mountains, etc.; cities that are not included as subject-entries and history and articles on miscellaneous subjects. The Editorial Board approved the Secretariat's "Proposed Plan," and agreed that work should start at once on the first three volumes, to be published by 1970, at least. Alphaeus, therefore, concentrated his efforts on work for Volume III. He relied on the assistance of the Cooperating Committees as the principal basis for the compilation of the biographical list of persons who played an important role in the political, cultural, economic and social history in Africa. He also sought advice of scholars specializing in the history of certain African countries.

By the end of 1965, the Secretariat had assembled a list of more than 1,400 names, with the historical figures of several countries yet to be included. The Standing Committee of the Editorial Board was to review the list and decide which names should be eliminated or added, and which authors should be invited to write the articles.

The volume of Alphaeus' work had tripled since his African tour, and he found himself increasingly burdened with a vast amount of night drudgery. From the very beginning, office help was never sufficient, and funds at his disposal were far too limited. Now that the plan had gained momentum, he felt the lack more keenly than ever. Patient and long suffering though he appeared, with a high frustration tolerance, nothing irritated him more and aroused his anger more than indolence and ineptitude in the work. He was a perfectionist. At home, he occasionally discussed it briefly, then shook his head in wordless displeasure.

I doubt that Alphaeus would have been content if he were not called upon for the depth of his strength. Others were less concerned. Under intense mental strain, he disregarded the fact that he owed a duty to himself as well as to others, and constantly abused his strength. His orderly mind would not permit neglected details or confusion of purpose. And his disciplined nature caused him to tackle more than he could safely manage, making him labor far beyond his endurance.

Such grave mental activity, late working hours and inadequate sleep brought on a heart attack, and Alphaeus was confined in the Military Hospital for a month in October 1964. For others, his voice always sounded strong and persistent, but for himself it was always mute. My concern for his health, however, would not permit me to remain silent, since no one seemed to be aware of the overpowering weight he assumed. I took advantage of the opportunity to talk with President Nkrumah during Alphaeus's confinement. Alphaeus would have vigorously opposed my discussion. Nkrumah admitted he really didn't know exactly what was going on, despite the Working Committee's assurance that he would be kept well informed.

"I'm here for that specific purpose," I said, "to bring you up to date on the conditions affecting Alphaeus." Nkrumah took notes, asked many questions, and promised to look into the matter, but months passed and nothing changed.

Before his illness, Alphaeus adhered to a tight routine, one that would eventually topple the strongest. At the stroke of six, and frequently before, his day started; by seven-thirty his long legs were trying to adjust to the small Skoda. Our big meal awaited him at noon, and after a brief rest, he returned to the office around two. Usually, between four-thirty and five the creaking gravel on the driveway announced his homecoming, and he immediately went to his study to work until supper, at seven. If there were no social engagements, he worked on into the night. Though the office closed on Saturday, his study never did.

A lover of bridge, Alphaeus never ceased to enjoy a good, serious game — remembering every card played and who played it. But occasions for such a break were not frequent. He was reluctant to spend many evenings away from his work. Fortunately, our veranda provided ample space for ping-pong, one of the few sports he enjoyed. And on Sundays, I insisted that he relax, if he did nothing more than beat me (as usual) at a swift, unmatched game that exercised him very little, but left me exhausted. His long arms and legs hardly moved while he smashed his deadly serves. It helped him to release the mounting tension and it pleased him to watch me frantically chasing the ball.

In the summer of 1965, China's Ambassador to Ghana, Mr. Huang Hua, now China's permanent delegate to the U.N., arranged for a visit for us to his country. En route, we stopped in Cairo for two days where Alphaeus conferred with officials at the Ministry of International Cultural Relations, and met again with Dr. Abdel-Malik Auda and Professor Ibrahim Sakr. During our one day stopover in Karachi, Pakistan, a bus ride into town was all we could manage. We were pleasantly surprised while walking down a narrow, crooked street, to meet a South African freedom fighter whom Alphaeus had known for some years.

Because of an approaching cyclone and subsequent tidal wave that killed over 12,000 people in East Pakistan, our plane detoured to that old colonial trading center, Rangoon, Burma, instead of landing in Dacca. The airport was so dimly lit we wondered how the Customs Officer expected us to fill out our papers. Passengers grumbled, but made the best of it. We eventually settled in the Strand Hotel, a once famous meeting place of the upper crust when the British Empire was at its height. It obviously had seen better days.

"Where is the Shive Dagon Pagoda?" Alphaeus asked an elderly man as we left the hotel for a walk. A colorful sarong, wrapped around his pathetically thin body and tied over his flat stomach, showed his protruding hip bones.

"Walk three blocks, turn to your right, walk four blocks, turn to your left...then turn..." The directions were endless, but we started out. All the detours more than made up for the spectacular sight of the largest and most famous Buddhist shrine in the world, dating back 2,500 years. One could spend an entire day watching the flow of people going up and down the wide stairs, some praying, some eating, and many just looking, as we were.

When our plane touched down in Shanghai, China's most populous city, four officials, two charming young girls with flowers, and our good friend Vicki Garvin met us. Vicki, an American Black who had gone to China from Ghana some months previous to teach English in the Institute of Foreign Languages, was dressed in a khaki pant suit, wore a Chinese haircut and cap, and for a moment I failed to recognize her.

Shanghai, a major base for aggressive activities of foreign countries in China for more than a hundred years, once reigned as mistress of the Orient, with unlimited privileges granted by China's Imperial Court. It was also a haven for gangsters, pickpockets, thugs, and hordes of beggars, particularly along the Whangpoo River enbankment. Now the city is one of the country's major commercial centers and the busiest port.

Our interpreter, Lui Hsian-Chang, arrived early next morning to escort us to the Pioneer's Palace in Yong Pu-Workers' District. Each day was crammed to capacity with visits to an industrial exhibition, Tang Yuan People's Commune, a self-sufficient unit twenty miles from Shanghai, and a host of other places of interest.

The city was alive with people, yet the streets were almost traffic-free. We were struck by the bubbling gaiety of the healthy children, who seemed to be everywhere. "It looks like a city of youth," Alphaeus commented. Young people dominated every scene, especially Nanking Road, Shanghai's shopping district, which boasted numerous specialty shops and large department stores.

Vicki's senior class brought back memories of Alphaeus' teaching years as he listened to her students. He found them very fluent in English, with good pronunciation, and an eagerness to demonstrate their ability. A lively discussion developed, relating to the Afro-Asian Conference and Blacks in the U.S. And they displayed a keen interest in the Encyclopedia Project. As one student remarked, "We will be waiting patiently for its production."

Mr. Lui Si Mu, Deputy Director of the Institute of International Relations, one of our hosts, accompanied us. He was well acquainted with Dr. Herbert Aptheker's writings and he later put many questions to Alphaeus. Finally, he asked, "Is he Negro?"

An afternoon of viewing the excellent displays of objects from the prehistoric to the exquisite creations of the latest Ching Dynasty in the Museum of Historical Art was an exciting prelude to the quiet evening with Talitha Gerlack. Vicki had arranged a dinner with Talitha, an American who knew Alphaeus' sister Eunice when they did Y.W.C.A. work in New York. Eunice, a lawyer and a staunch, conservative Republican, had served as assistant District Attorney to Thomas Dewey, District Attorney of New York. She bitterly opposed Alphaeus' Marxist views, and for years his politics estranged them. Talitha quoted Eunice, saying, "Sometimes I think he took the right path." Jerry Tannenbaum and his lovely Chinese wife soon joined the group and added their sparkle to the discussions that continued until midnight.

The day before our departure, Alphaeus spent the greater part of the afternoon with three members of the Shanghai Academy of Social Sciences, Mr. Yao Nai, Vice President, Mr. Pu Tseng-Yuan, Scientific Secretary, and Mr. Shen Yi-Sing, Deputy Director of the Research Institute of History. He explained his work on the Encyclopedia and some aspects of African history. It was a long and drawn out meeting, since the discussion had to be translated, and Alphaeus wondered how much had been correctly interpreted. Nevertheless, his hosts showed genuine interest by their pointed questions. They did not think five years too long for publishing the first three volumes.

Flying low leaving Shanghai, one saw vast stretches of rice paddies along with tidy gray and green patches around numerous clusters of villages. Not an inch of space was wasted. A welcoming party of six men and two women with flowers met us in Peking, and though it was two a.m., we went to a private V.I.P. lounge and remained for a long time, exchanging compliments and courtesies.

En route to the city, on the long, perfectly straight, tree-lined road that merged into T-ien-am Men Square, we passed several mule drawn carts piled high with what looked like hay. Silently, bringing up the rear, were a few energetic cyclists laden with freshly cut vegetables for the open market. The Gates of Heavenly Peace of the once Forbidden City, etched in light, lent stateliness to the square where Mao Tse-tung reviewed the October first parade, and 100,000 people assemble with ease.

The new and the old mingle in Peking, the capital of the Peoples' Republic of China. The country's main center of science and culture swarms with six million people. Wherever we went, the curious but friendly Chinese surrounded us with looks of inquisitiveness. When we learned to say **"Ni-hao"** (hello), their stares immediately changed into broad smiles.

As in Shanghai, Alphaeus met with several members of Academia Sinica, Mr. Hsia Nai, Director of the Institute of Archaeology, Mr. Sung Shu Li, Chief of Liaison, and Mr. Chang You Yu, Deputy Director of the Department of Philosophy and Social Sciences. He was pleased to have discussions with the Vice-Chairman of the Editorial Board of **China Reconstructs**, Mr. Tang Ming-Chao, and especially with the Director of the Institute of Afro-Asian Studies, Mr. Wu Chou Chen.

The invitation to China was not merely for sightseeing and getting to know the Chinese people, as important as that was, but also for Alphaeus' health. For four days we visited various places of interest, attended the ballet, and dined sumptuously with our six hosts who represented various departments of the Academia Sinica, and the Institute of International Relations. Then we checked in at Peking Union Hospital, that we learned was run by American Missions in imperial days and served only the wealthy and Europeans. Alphaeus needed treatment for his heart condition, and I hoped some kind of therapy would relieve my arthritic hands and shoulder. Ten days of acupuncture and moxibustion (burning of herbs over affected parts), brought me considerable relief while Alphaeus underwent tests and treatment.

The doctors decided Alphaeus needed more rest, and we left with two interpreters for Tsingtao, on the Yellow Sea. The long train ride provided an opportunity to observe the countryside in the early morning hours. Workers were already in the fields by five a.m. They cultivated the land to the edge of the railroad, around gravestones, and sculptured the hills by incalculable human toil. Few people paused to look at the passing train. They were too busy pulling and carrying in place of motor power. The young attendants in charge of each car looked more like school girls with their long braids and bows. They kept the cars scrupulously clean, and at each long stop the cars were washed.

The Director of Tsingtao Sanatorium, Dr. Jen Tong, and others met us and we were installed in a newly furbished house. Two days later we were moved to a more imposing one (just vacated by another patient) despite our protest. Alphaeus' interpreter, Wu Chang, told him that only the most respected comrade visitors were invited to Tsingtao, and they wanted him to have the best. The long years of foreign occupation (Japanese, German, French and English), were evident in the various types of architecture, particularly the houses, though the extensive industrial area on the outskirts seemed rather drab.

Alphaeus' medical checkup showed a slow heartbeat, and Dr. Lui Shih Deh advised him to take it easy. Every afternoon, after our morning ritual, a half-hour instruction in shadow boxing in the garden; my acupuncture by the venerable Dr. Liu Ku Ri, who taught acupuncture in the sanatorium, and Alphaeus' massage, we took off to see some interesting sights. Our visit to the Workers' Sanatorium (one of five in Tsingtao), where patients come from all over China for physio-therapy treatment for three to six months, was most revealing. Some patients spoke excellent English and did not hesitate to speak of their dreadful experiences before the revolution. Their stories brought tears to my eyes.

One evening, Dr. Jen came over to chat, and as we were teaching our interpreters bridge, he was eager to join.

"Where did you learn to play bridge?" Alphaeus asked.

"Twenty years ago at Yenan, from Dr. Norman Bethune," he replied. "But I haven't played since."

Dr. Bethune, a famous Canadian thoracic surgeon, one of the highest-paid persons in his profession, and a Communist, abandoned his practice and went to Spain to help the Republic in 1936. He set up the first mobile blood banks. The last two years of his life (1937-1939), however he spent with the Chinese Red Army that finally found shelter at the end of that epic 6,000 mile "Long March" in the hand carved caves in the dry hills of Yenan. When time permitted one to relax from the horrors of war, Dr. Jen had learned bridge. He played surprisingly well, despite the lapse in time. And with each succeeding hand his enthusiasm grew. He was so pleased with the chance to play again that two hours passed before he realized he was due at the sanatorium. For Alphaeus, it was a joy to watch his partner wrinkle his brow, scratch his chin in consternation and finally make the right bid.

Back in Peking after ten days in Tsingtao, we took a small plane for Siam, in the northwest. A city of great antiquity and culture, it nevertheless displayed in many areas, the new wave of life. The heat hit us like a ball of fire when we arrived, but the huge, empty hotel, built for Soviet technicians, seemed cool. No visiting Chinese stayed there. They used another dormitory. Of singular interest to us was the Emperor's hot springs palace, a fabulous place, a long ride out of the city, where Chiang Kaishek was arrested by patriotic Koumintang generals.

After three days of activity, we moved on to Loyang by overnight train, but not before Alphaeus was given another checkup.

Again we lodged in the hotel provided for Soviet technicians. It had a swimming pool and basketball court. How we longed for a swim in that oppressive heat, but we didn't have the nerve to ask.

The tour of Lungmen Caves — huge Buddhist statues on a cliff beside a river — impressed us, but not nearly as much as the Special Primary School. Serious young students were making radio sets, bottling cough medicine of their own manufacture. One class was busy sending and receiving wireless messages — unusual school activities for small children.

Three days after our return to Peking, Alphaeus gave a talk to the Afro-Asian group at the Academy of Sciences. Questions on the Encyclopedia were so numerous that the Director had to call a halt after three hours. Alphaeus was completely spent, but glad to have had the occasion to bring the students and members up to date on some vital issues.

An evening dinner arranged by Tang Ming-Chao of **China Reconstructs** and Sol Adler, with about twenty of the American community, completely offset the hectic morning. All the Americans were either teachers or polishers of English. The event tingled with lively topics, old American songs and toasts. One American, after toasting several people, places and things, sang out with fervor "To Brooklyn, without any qualifications." That called for a loud hurrah, since several Brooklynites were there, including us.

There were still many things to see. The Great Wall, built twenty-two centuries ago to keep out the barbarian invaders from the north, was less difficult to climb than Alphaeus expected. Along with viewing the ex-cavated tomb of one of the thirteen Ming emperors, who lie in a peaceful valley, surrounded by lofty mountains, it was an impressive finale to our excursion.

Our farewell gathering in a special dining room of the Congress Hall of the People, with the Vice-Minister of Propaganda and those associated with our visit, was a banquet that overwhelmed us. Before and after din-ner the officials truly put Alphaeus on the spot with their sharp questions and lively discussions. The affair was long but enjoyable, with the usual toast, the men downing that very potent liquor, **mao-t-ai,** made from sorghum.

It took us many days to sort out the incredible events and intensely human encounters and feelings we shared in that alluring country. We learned a great deal about the hard working, long suffering Chinese. Stoic patience helped them to handle their difficulties with confidence, and gave them courage to endure.

"Conscious pride in what China has accomplished — by her own ef-forts," Alphaeus wrote to a friend, "showed in their enthusiasm for their changing lives and their cheerful good humor that reflected a sense of freedom from intimidation." An illuminating adventure, the trip added an extra dimension to our lives.

Chinese delegates and others going to Helsinki to the World Peace meeting completely filled the plane to Moscow, and there was little gaiety on the long, twelve hour trip. The brief stopover at Irkutsk and Omsk gave one a chance to see how bleak and uninviting the far north can be. Alphaeus surmised that the Soviet Embassy in Peking apparently had not forwarded his information, as there was no one at the airport to meet us. That disturbed him, and he finally alerted a woman attendant to phone the Academy. After waiting an hour and a half, Irena, our interpreter on a previous visit, came running to greet us.

We became aware that some changes had occurred since our last visit when the taxi driver asked Alphaeus for eighty kopecks, more than a dollar, to take our four bags to our hotel room. We had thought the "no tipping" rule was still in effect. Not so with that driver.

To meet old friends, to reminisce over past events, and exchange ideas for improved relations between people is always refreshing. We did just that between Alphaeus' three conferences and his talk to the students at Africa Institute. We learned how steadily the standard of living had improved. Much of it was evident in the fashionably dressed women in the street and the increase and variety of consumer goods, except cars. Queues for food-stuffs and other basic articles had virtually disappeared.

Of special interest to Alphaeus was his visit with Professor Dmitri Olderogge of the Institute d'Ethnographie, Academy of Sciences in Leningrad. He recalled some of Olderogge's enlightening views about the historical background and development of African languages in 1959, on the occasion of our first trip to the Soviet Union. He was pleased with the opportunity to discuss with him again some pertinent subjects. Our visit to his country home, not far from Leningrad, provided a perfect setting for a quiet, relaxing afternoon.

Paris had always fascinated Alphaeus, and he insisted that we stop there and in London on our way home. Now a seasoned traveler, he delighted in new circumstances and challenges. Since he had a few days left from his leave, Beirut was added to the list.

The question of the appointment of a director for the Encyclopedia Africana had been raised a number of times, and the Secretariat had attempted to secure names of candidates from a few of those closely associated with the Secretariat locally. Members from the Standing Committee of the Editorial Board had also been approached. The results were negative, and there was only one recommended prospect.

In November 1965, the Standing Committee met at the University of Ghana to review the work accomplished by the Secretariat during the past year. They arrived at several important decisions affecting the future development of the project. Present at the meeting under the chairmanship of Professor W.E. Abraham, Pro-Vice Chancellor of the University of Ghana, were Professor A. Bouhdiba of Tunisia; Dr. S. O. Biobaku, Vice-Chancellor of the University of Lagos; Dr. W. K. Chagula, Principal of the University College Tanzania; Dr. Ibrahim Sakr of Cairo University; Mr. Mario de Andrade of Angola, and Professor Mekki Shibeika of the University of Khartoum.

The Standing Committee decided unanimously that Alphaeus, who had been serving as Secretary, should be appointed to fill the vacancy of Director. They also agreed that Mr. L. W. Hesse, Research Officer, should be appointed Chief Administrator, performing the functions of Secretary. The permanent headquarters should be in Accra, and the work of the preparation and printing of the Arabic edition should be centered in Cairo. A final decision on the center for preparing the French edition was postponed pending correspondence with the Secretariat's collaborators in French-speaking African countries.

Immediately after the meeting, the General Secretary of the Ghana Academy of Sciences, Dr. J. Yanney-Ewisie, sent Alphaeus a message: "Any recommendations by the Standing Committee of the Editorial Board of the Encyclopedia Africana regarding the post of Director for the Encyclopedia Secretariat should not be given publicity, since the appointment of Directors of institutes is made by the Praesidium of the Ghana Academy of Sciences, to which any such recommendations should be referred."

The Ghana Academy of Sciences completely ignored the decision of the Standing Committee to appoint Alphaeus Director, but searched around to find a Ghanaian to fill the post. It didn't matter that Alphaeus had drawn up the plan, directed the work, and labored to the point of exhaustion for four years. The mind-shattering job eventually made him ill from overwork. The fact that twenty-five years of scholarly research and dedicated activity had made him an outstanding Africanist seemed not to have entered the picture.

Two Ghanaian professors declined the position, but the Academy later found Professor L.H. Ofosu-Appiah disposed to taking over the reins of the Secretariat.

Professor Ofosu-Appiah was teaching Latin and Greek at Dartmouth College and knew absolutely nothing about the work. Yet in August, Alphaeus was confronted with his new Director. Africans frequently resent seeing foreigners in jobs they feel should be filled by countrymen Perhaps that was a factor in Alphaeus' case. But, was the Academy really concerned with the efficiency and progress of the Encyclopedia when it made such a drastic change?

March 1966, marked the end of Alphaeus's four year contract. His application for renewal offered him an appointment as Area Editor. He would be stripped of all responsibilities for the administration of the Encyclopedia. Those duties were transferred to Mr. Hesse. This was not only an unmistakable insult to his intelligence, but a shock and humiliation. Alphaeus knew that it took strength, not weakness to compromise. Though the shift hurt him deeply, and caused him to wonder about the future of the Encyclopedia, he was too devoted to his task, and too eager to get on with the job to permit his personal discontent to interfere with the work. He accepted without bitterness the contract terms of one tour of fifteen months, subject to renewal on the production of a Medical Certificate of fitness after the tour.

Alphaeus said little during the ensuing days, but retreated into a silence so loud you could hear its stillness. Solitude never seemed to leave his spirit. A brooding isolation became his natural state. My angry discussions on the topic he quickly discouraged, and I soon let the issue lie, knowing how bitterly he detested arguments. The dark intensity of his countenance reenforced the fact of his eternal preoccupation with weighty affairs. He was quite unaware of holding his left hand tightly clenched while walking or standing, and expressed surprise when I called it to his attention. To me it indicated clearly a manifestation of an inward tightness that he was unable to release.

The formal opening of the Volta River Dam at Akosombo, that harnessed the Volta River flow and converted it into valuable hydro-electric power, was inaugurated in 1966. It was now possible for the government to make giant strides forward in economic development. But, on February 24, a military coup struck Ghana, deposed Kwame Nkrumah, and shattered his dreams of a prosperous country. The people were stunned.

We could scarcely believe our ears when shots rang out in the early morning hours. Alphaeus jumped out of bed and ran to the window. Another shot pierced the air. He turned on the radio. No sound! Finally, a little after six, a voice, cold and abrupt, announced the takeover of the government by the Ghanaian Armed Forces and the police. We were dumbfounded.

After two days, when all was quiet on the Accra front, and police barriers were taken down, Alphaeus went to the office. It was a day of distress. The office was across the street from Kanda Estate, the homes of many security officers. Like Kanda Estate, it was a wreck. There were many bullet holes; locks on doors had been forced; the contents of drawers had been dumped on the floor, and steel cabinets pried open. Of course the petty-cash box was gone, along with a typewriter, some furniture and other articles. A few days later the staff were ordered out and settled in another section.

Ghana, the country that started all Africa down freedom road; once the inspiration of Blacks and a haven for the oppressed from many parts of

Africa, groaned under her betrayal. The nation of fantastic progress amid mounting obstacles was home to many young Afro-Americans who formed a large, active community. They were among the first to be deported.

Nine months after the coup, while we sat on the veranda with friends in the early evening of November seventeenth, a young messenger handed Alphaeus a note. As he read, a look of desperation, then despair, clouded his face. He stood there dejected, the small paper hanging limp between his fingers, and a vacant stare in his half-closed eyes.

I sprang to my feet, bewildered, exclaiming, "What is it?"

Alphaeus seemed in a state of shock, totally and completely undone. It took some time before he could speak. He handed me the paper and slowly sat down.

"We are being deported," he said.

Mortified and embarrassed, he hung his head and said nothing more, but took refuge in discreet silence. I looked at the paper in disbelief. "...you are therefore warned to leave Ghana forthwith, and in any event not later than the 26th November, 1966." A numbness crept over me as the full impact of the message registered. Like a dying man who views his entire life in a flash of vivid recollections, Alphaeus' struggling years with the Encyclopedia swept through my mind, like lightning, and I saw **red.** My mind must have snapped for the moment, for I went into such a rage that Alphaeus had to hold me down. The poor messenger, who took the brunt of my fury, stood petrified, tears running down his cheeks. Our friends, equally stunned, could find no words to express their dismay, and soon left us to our grief. Nine days to leave the country!

The only warning we had of anything amiss had been on August 25th, when three men from the Special Branch of the Police searched Alphaeus' office and our home, looking for — what? We could never find out. Since "nothing incriminating was found," according to the investigator, Alphaeus was never called in for questioning, and everything went along quietly for three months. One investigator, while going through my mail, asked if we were in contact with Nkrumah, who was then in Guinea. They knew we had lived there for two years. Perhaps they expected to find a note from him. But, why to us?

For days Alphaeus tried, without success, to get an interview with officials of the National Liberation Council. No one would see him. Nor could any of our friends discover the reason for our deportation. Our impression was that the Ghana authorities were eager to avoid any publicity, since not a single word about us appeared in the local press up to the day we left, or thereafter. Inasmuch as daily acounts of other deportees were flashed across the newspapers, it appeared strange. The story certainly would have embarrassed the N.L.C.

Time **was** short to crate a houseful of belongings, and we were getting desperate. As a last resort to get someone to intercede for us, I approached the priest at Holy Spirit Cathedral, an Afro-American, the Rev. Lawrence Thornton. For some time I had headed an international group of women who met once a week to sew for the poor in the church's community rooms. I knew that Mr. A.K. Deku, Commissioner of Police, C.I.D., was a member of the parish. As he had ignored Alphaeus' request for a meeting, perhaps Rev. Thornton could help. He was shocked when I told him the news, and immediately called Deku for an appointment. Deku declined to discuss the issue, but granted us five more days.

Air passage had already been arranged for us, but we refused to leave our possessions behind, and requested departure by boat. The S.S. African Lightning (Farrell Line), which soon docked, insisted it was taking no passengers, but the N.L.C. commandeered the freighter, and there was nothing they could do but take us aboard.

An interesting angle of the case came to light when our good friend Dr. Robert Lee, an Afro-American dentist, called on the U.S. Ambassador Franklin Williams on our behalf. Dr. Lee, a resident of Ghana for many years, with his wife Sarah, also a dentist, and their two sons, knew Williams well. They were college mates. Williams denied that he had anything to do with our deportation but he had seen our names on the list. Why should he see such a list of another country? Did the N.L.C. compile it, or the C.I.A. of the U.S.A.? Our banishment was concrete evidence of the military government's lack of self-assurance, and a bid to keep in the good graces of the Neo-Colonialists.

"It is particularly disgraceful," wrote Kwame Nkrumah in **Dark Days in Ghana,** that it should have been an Afro-American ambassador who sold himself out to the imperialists and allowed himself to be used... It was the same man who deliberately lied when he publicly described the coup as bloodless."

The single thing that occupied all of Alphaeus' time, thought and energy for four and a half years had come to an abrupt end. Though it had been a rich and very rewarding experience, to be rudely cut off from the work one had shaped and watched grow over the years was painful. "It is like suddenly losing one's beloved child," he told a friend. If he could not complete the remaining months of his appointment contract, he had hoped, at least, to be allowed sufficient time to properly wind up his work and arrange for an orderly transfer. Alphaeus found it difficult to understand why that could not have been done. Why the sudden rush to get rid of him? What distressed him most was the utter lack of concern for the consequences of the hasty termination upon the continuity of the Encyclopedia, as well as the callous disregard for the most elementary principles of justice.

Had there been time to make preparations we would have preferred to take up residence in another African country, rather than return to New York. Alphaeus was not interested in returning to New York, though he had been away six and a half years. He wanted to remain in Africa. Wherever he would be, he stood ready to assist in whatever way possible toward the achievement of the goals set by the Encyclopedia board.

That the project had in fact assumed a truly Pan-African character, one of its objectives was especially attested by the endorsement given it by the Organization of African Unity. Alphaeus could take some satisfaction in the knowledge that he had succeeded in accomplishing a great deal against tremendous odds. What with the acute shortage of skilled manpower, because seasoned scholars are in high demand, a distinguished group of collaborators had been assembled.

In his letter terminating Alphaeus' appointment, the General Secretary of the Ghana Academy of Sciences wrote: "I wish to convey, on behalf of the Academy and without prejudice to the reasons that led to the action of the government, the gratitude of the Academy to you for the contribution you made to keep the Encyclopedia Africana on its feet from the date of your assumption of duty to the present."

Considering how furtively the Academy pulled the rug out from under his feet by not permitting Alphaeus to assume the office of Director (he had filled the post unofficially from the beginning) and deliberately demoting him, the gratitude seemed rather hollow. But he made no comment.

In the concluding paragraph of a long article on Alphaeus' expulsion in the **Afro-American,** January 3, 1967, Charles P. Howard, the noted U.N. correspondent, wrote:

> ...The dismissal of Dr. Hunton and the way it was done certainly was not designed to improve the quality of the Encyclopedia Africana. The gathering and recording of the history of Africa is a project of great importance to the people of Africa and to the people of African descent all over the world.
>
> The colonialists and imperialists who have falsified the history of the African and who have lied about the contributions of great Africans to the arts and sciences of the world don't want the Encyclopedia African published.
>
> Once again the so-called Liberation Council is doing the bidding of its white masters and destroying Ghana's contribution to Africa and to the peoples of African descent. Kicking Afro-Americans of great talent out of Ghana serves the colonialist and imperialist, not Ghanaians and Africans.

---

12. ZAMBIA: LAST YEARS

Heavy of heart, we scarcely noticed the striking beauty of the calm ocean as we paced the deck and watched Tema's busy harbor receding in the distance. With his long, black pipe clenched tensely between his teeth, and his dark eyes filled with melancholy, Alphaeus lost himself in thought. He seemed devastated. The years of struggle to live in tune with his inner, governing force and idealism, against mounting uncertainties and crushing odds, had etched his countenance with a strangely foreboding expression. Unselfishly, and with love, he had given so much of himself through the years, but he received so little for his strenuous efforts.

My heart ached for what man's inhumanity to man had done to him. Would the human heart ever overpower the scheming mind and bring harmony out of chaos? I knew that at this critical juncture, Alphaeus would never open up and give vent to those locked-in feelings. He kept them as secure as in a vault.

Unable to speak, I put my trembling hand in his, while we continued to walk. His long, slender fingers gripped mine. So many of our shared experiences had been rich and compensating. Now, courage dropped low, and hope reached its ebb. "When sorrows come," wrote Shakespeare, "they come not single but in battalions." Life is conditioned, to be sure, but certainly not fated. Another door closed abruptly behind us. Tomorrow would come, despite its dimness, and perhaps with it, renewed hope. Gradually, the sun dipped into the Atlantic, and beautiful Ghana, once so gay and full of vitality and promise, slipped quietly out of sight.

The month-long trip afforded ample time for reflection, and no excitement except the Christmas celebration with the Captain and his mates. Since we were the only passengers, days passed slowly. We had nothing to do but read and write in the library. A stop-over in Monrovia, Liberia, to take on a cargo of raw rubber from the well-known Firestone rubber plantation, however, gave Alphaeus a chance to visit Dr. Abeodu B. Jones, with the Bureau of African and Asian Affairs, of the Department of State, who was a member of the Editorial Board.

With relieved anxiety, we watched the high gales subside as New York's shore came into view. For two days, the wind blew with such fury that the ship lifted and ducked, swayed and rocked, knocking everything over that was not screwed down. Still the bitter January wind continued to pierce us through and through. We were somewhat irritated, though not overly surprised when our freighter, instead of stopping in New York as we expected, landed us and our crates along with the rubber consignment at Fall River, Massachusetts, where a Firestone processing plant is located. It meant extra, unexpected expense to transport our goods to New York.

Alphaeus had mixed feelings about being in the U.S. "I feel restless, like a fish out of water," he told Alan S. Oser of the **New York Times** in an interview at my sister's home in Staten Island. "There is an openness in Africa, spatial as well as imaginative, which is not present in a sophisticated place like New York." He had not been embittered by the adversities in Ghana after the coup, but he had tried to maintain a proper perspective on the convulsions taking place in Africa. Though he didn't think "they had anything against him personally, it was unnerving and humiliating."

Alphaeus did not want disastrous circumstances, which he could not control, to shape his life, and crush his spirit. He strove to see the better side of people, and believed in their innate goodness, notwithstanding his own hardships. Most of all, he loved his work and wanted to devote the rest of his life to its completion. Yet to do the little things that others frequently left undone annoyed him, he required peace and harmony in his surroundings, almost at any price, and he left no stone unturned to adjust matters when they went wrong. Always he used tact and diplomacy, rather than force. Concern for offending others ran deep.

One of the important features of the work Alphaeus missed stemmed from the influx of knowledge received from various contributors, which made fascinating reading. He also felt the loss of the country's spirit, its friendliness and struggle for progress. Despite the divergence of ideas and identification with the nation's problems, the personal involvement of the people had excited him.

He realized that much of Africa's past is kept alive by word of mouth, one generation passing information on to the next. This, of course, increased the urgency to collect the history. At the rate young people were leaving elders and migrating to cities in droves, it would take only about one generation for orally transmitted stories of the past to be forgotten and irrevocably lost as history.

The continuation of the Encyclopedia gave him deep concern. He hoped the work would go on, and that he might be able to join it again. In the meantime, he kept in touch with many scholars in the thirty-two African countries, who were terribly disturbed over his ouster.

"Alas!" wrote one professor, "the U.S. has found a second real foothold in West Africa, i.e. in addition to Liberia... I am really saddened that the work of the Encyclopedia has come to an end. This is another triumph for the Neo-Colonial forces in Africa." The professor was particularly upset because, as he put it, "this means in effect that U.N.E.S.C.O.'s official history of Africa under the direction of Dr. K. O. Dike will now proceed without any possibility of a countervailing body of evidence and interpretation." As a member of the Board, he expressed the sentiments of many collaborators when he said Alphaeus' departure was "an immense loss to all of us." Nevertheless he could rest assured that they appreciated the effort and direction he gave to the Encyclopedia.

The winds of change, blowing like a tempest over the country, continued to gain velocity when we returned. Black youths marching and demonstrating had lit the flame of revolt, and the blaze continued to spread, particularly in the South, where the focal point of national unrest had reached an intensified level. Blacks had had enough. Their frustrations and broodings would no longer stifle their ambitions and corrode their souls. They fought back — not always wisely, nor with tactics involving intelligence and skill. Yet fight back they would, with the fear of death no hindrance.

In his speech, "Tribute to William L. Patterson" on his 75th birthday, at the Americana Hotel in January 1967, Alphaeus remarked how reassured he and many others had been in Ghana to read about the invasion of the army recruiting center in Atlanta, Georgia, by Black youths with picket signs reading, "No Viet Cong ever called me a nigger," and the picket demonstration a year before in Newark, in protest against the so-called Brotherhood Award to the American tycoon, Charles Engelhard, who garnered millions in profits annually from cheap labor of thousands of exploited black workers in the gold and other mining properties owned or controlled by his corporation in South Africa.

Alphaeus believed that more and bigger demonstrations were required in the face of the crisis then in Rhodesia and the even more ominous crisis looming in South Africa. He admonished the audience to have no doubts about the ultimate outcome of the African revolution, or waver in their firm support of their African allies because of the setbacks suffered by progressive forces in one African country or another. To lack confidence in them was to lack confidence in themselves. Optimism still permeated the action in new Africa, despite the predictions of ill fate stacked against her. "Have courage!" he said. "Whatever the maneuvers of those who desperately strive to turn back the clock in Africa, and to sidetrack the developing political consciousness of the Black masses in America and prevent the fulfillment of their insistent demands, the movement forward of both Africans, and Afro-Americans is irreversible. It is irreversible because, as Dr. Du Bois said, 'it is the rise of these people that is the rise of the world.' "

Speaking invitations poured in, soon after our arrival. The Detroit Federation of Teachers wanted Alphaeus to address their conference on Racism in Education. The Columbia University Seminar on Contemporary Africa requested a talk on the Encyclopedia project - to name only two. Yet he was to busy trying to find a way of returning to Africa to prepare speeches, though he accepted a few engagements.

A meeting with Zambia's Minister of Foreign Affairs, Mr. Simon Kapwepwe, who was at the U.N., brought promising results. In February, the President of the Republic of Zambia, Dr. Kenneth Kaunda, who remembered Alphaeus at Accra, invited us to Zambia as his guests. He would then explore the possibility of Alphaeus's continuation with his important work.

Alphaeus was elated over the generous offer, and looked forward to a permanent residence or an extended stay. His natural eagerness to get back to the project, if at all feasible, the President knew, but he assured him that he was prepared, as an alternative, to consider any appointment within his competence. Due to his commitments Alphaeus could not leave within the month, as we were asked to do, but on the first of May, we flew to Lusaka, the capital of Zambia. Filled with anticipation of a new beginning in a new country, we looked forward to many interesting and untried experiences.

While shouts went up and cries of "Freedom" echoed through the crowd, the leaders of that young Central African Republic, Zambia, knew that their troubles had just begun. For nearly seventy years, Britain saw no need to develop her protectorate, Northern Rhodesia, beyond the stage of mining her vast raw materials for American and British industries. The copperbelt ore "is so rich, and the labor so cheap," the **Wall Street Journal's** correspondent reported (August 8, 1953) "that producers can reduce prices 50 percent below the U.S. break-even point, and still make money." Rhodesian copper was big business. Although the entire economy is based on mining, mainly copper, lead and zinc, Britain processed none locally, nor did the country benefit in exchange for the raw exports.

The reins of government changed into African hands on October 24th, 1964, and Zambia's immediate concern was not only how to raise the starvation wage standard of some 40,000 miners who produced the wealth, but a meager agricultural economy. The organized mine workers of Northern Rhodesia had a long history of struggle for wages, and against the whites-always-on-top employment systems, as far back as 1935, when six Africans were killed in the suppression of a strike.

Unlike Ghana, Zambia had a very large community of European settlers. Before independence, nearly 50,000 resided within her landlocked borders. Many came from South Africa and Southern Rhodesia and brought their apartheid hatreds with them. They farmed some of the eighty million acres of land suitable for cultivation (one of the highest potentials in Africa), supervised the mines, owned the commerce, ran the government, and, of course the Africans.

As Alphaeus pointed out in **Decisions in Africa,** Zambia is the third largest producer of copper after the U.S. and the U.S.S.R., and the leading exporter of the metal. Her fortunes are bound to copper, which accounts for 95 percent of the country's export earnings. As copper goes, so goes Zambia. A fluctuating market could spell disaster.

Walking down Cairo Road, in Lusaka, the main commercial district, one had the impression of being in some moderate size provincial town in Europe or the U.S. This was particularly true when we drove through the residential section, "low density area" where most whites lived and a few Africans. Their elegant homes surrounded by lush gardens of hibiscus, bougainvillea, and other tropical plant life revealed a striking contrast to the inevitable "high density area" with crudely or unpaved streets where the majority of the Africans lived crowded together. They left much to be desired.

President Kaunda welcomed us at an informal dinner in the State House, several days after our arrival, and from then on, Alphaeus had a difficult time trying to get an appointment to talk over his stay. Something always interfered. We felt rather embarrassed living in the Guest Lodge on the State House grounds where, in the beginning, security guards checked us in and out. The over-pampered service by the staff, a hangover from the British, at times made us feel guilty, and a bit uneasy.

A month passed, and still no word from the President. Alphaeus knew he was leaving on an extended trip to India, Pakistan and China, and he didn't welcome the continued lack of activity. In desperation, he wrote to Kaunda expressing his desire to be of service. The President was deeply touched by his "wanting to be on the move with and in Zambia," and asked him to look into the problem of alcoholism, during his absence, and suggest how they might fight it.

Actually, Kaunda wanted time to investigate further whether there was anything Alphaeus could do to help the Encyclopedia project. When he returned, Mr. Amando Yeta, who had the responsibility for organizing and leading the cooperating Committee in striking Zambia, went to Accra to inquire. Zambia did not recognize Ghana's military government and the trip accomplished nothing. Meanwhile, Alphaeus continued his investigation into the constantly growing hazard of beer drinking.

In Zambia, where maize is a staple, the home brew is a thick, sweetish beer called **chubuka.** Although commercial beer has made a great impact on urban Africa, it's a luxury for many. Most Africans in the rural and poorer urban areas continue to drink the cheaper brew. As elsewhere in Africa, alcoholism has become a major social problem in the cities where the crowded beer halls in the midst of African compounds have flourished.

Because the President saw no possibility of Alphaeus resuming his work on the Encyclopedia in the near future, he arranged for him to undertake research on the history of the Nationalist Movement in Zambia, under the Kenneth Kaunda Foundation. The planned proposal would take four or five years to complete. Alphaeus immediately began a survey of what thus far had been written in order to determine what the priorities for further research should be. He also felt it was essential to have the services of a suitable Zambian scholar for the purpose of conducting or actively participating in the work of interviewing and assembling information from individual Zambians who may have first-hand knowledge of facts or events requiring investigation.

Long before independence, Zambian leaders realized their educational system required rebuilding. And to that end, the Kenneth Kaunda Foundation was founded in 1966. It has three main objectives: to achieve complete Zambian production of all primary (and later secondary) school books; to distribute all school supplies and encourage their manufacture within Zambia, and to use the profits for scholarships and other development projects. To promote those aims the Foundation formed two companies: The National Education Company of Zambia — concerned with publishing of books for school, and those of general interest, and the National Education Distribution Company of Zambia Ltd., which handles all distribution of everything the classroom needs.

The housing shortage in Lusaka, as well as in other cities, was a source of legitimate worry to the government. It caused us to stay in the Guest Lodge for six months before a house could be found. Though we lived comfortably, time weighed heavily on my hands. There's a limit to sitting around with nothing to do. At the end of the first month, I volunteered to teach English and dressmaking to the wives of the State House staff. A small house, which the social worker used to give lessons in nutrition and sewing, became my classroom.

I made several word charts, bought books and with six illiterate women as students, started to teach. Their eagerness to learn those marvelous skills, reading and writing, increased each day. The class quickly outgrew the room. Despite the noise of babies crying, nursing and burping, while mothers grappled with the big, black letters on the wall, the results proved gratifying. To see an elderly woman, dignified and prim in her freshly pressed dress, suddenly look up from her notebook with excitement in her eyes, when she realizes for the first time that she can write her name, was a genuine thrill. Lena, a grandmother, was my best student, and slowly progressed to the point where some words in the newspaper took on meaning. What a sensation! One wondered about all the talent that perhaps lay hidden in those thwarted and defrauded humans. A new world opens up to one who can read, even though he or she may be handicapped by an impoverished culture and educational background. I regretted leaving my students when we moved. They taught me far more then I taught them.

For Alphaeus, there were no exciting pressures of a busy, new life to offset the steadily eroding effects of increasing frustrations. Nevertheless, he immersed himself in his latest assignment, became totally involved, and gave it none but his best. The taunting memories of spirited discussions with colleagues, and continued isolation from his cherished work, brought a gradual withdrawal into injured despondency. He rarely discussed our crude expulsion from Ghana. An affable front, and a nicely blended intellectual and emotional nature, however, could not shield from me the inner turmoil I sensed as communication became more labored. In his quiet, reserved manner, he seemed strangely removed from Zambian life, except in those brief encounters with friends. At home his silence distressed me. I tried to make him understand that one of life's keys is to share with affection all the woes that burdens one's heart; to talk it out, let the air blow through, and then let the rest take care of itself with time. It seldom worked.

This was yet another instance when I became acutely aware that regardless of my ability to understand with depth and sensitivity, in certain ways Alphaeus and I remained strangers, even though we had grown to know each other well. After many years of intimate living, this complicated person I loved continued to elude any probing. It puzzled and disturbed me as it did in other moments of crisis. Only love provided motivation to accept it with grace. Some problems even love cannot solve, for every man is indeed an island, though many may disagree.

Lusaka was far less stimulating intellectually and culturally than Accra, due to the repressive influence of the dominant European settlers. The speed and effectiveness with which the African could adjust to his new, emerging society depended to a great extent on what the past had made him. In certain segments of the population, some still suffered from a **Bwana** (master) complex. They find it difficult to free themselves from old habits, and must continually look over their shoulders for the white man's approval.

Social activities were rare. One depended to a great extent on small gatherings of friends and acquaintances. Yet, occasional Embassy affairs, foreign films at the Cinema Club, and from time to time, a play at the small theatre, made life more pleasant. We spent many lively Sundays by the pool of our good friends, the Barney Gordons. Every Sunday resembled open house. Barney Gordon, one of many whites who identified themselves for years with the South African national liberation movement, had lived in Zambia with his wife and daughter since 1963.

We met in 1945 when Barney, a staunch enthusiast of the Council on African Affairs and a member of the progressive ex-servicemen's organization, the Springbok Legion, came to New York with his wife, Sonia. Ever since, we had kept in touch. Because of Barney's activities on behalf of Africans, South Africa and later Southern Rhodesia deported him. Yet he continued to lend assistance from Zambia. Their friendship and thoughtfulness did much to ease our adjustment to Zambian life. This was abundantly clear when thieves stripped Alphaeus of nearly every stitch of clothing, except his shoes (they were much too large for any Zambian). The one special event of the year, a dinner dance at the University, gave the robbers ample time to make a clean sweep. Though my loss was considerable, I regretted most the stolen articles from China, which were irreplaceable.

Alphaeus occasionally met with a few freedom fighters, mostly from South Africa, who passed in and out of Lusaka. Zambia gave every possible support to the nationalist organizations dedicated to liberating the white minority-controlled areas. In June 1968, he started a series of articles, "A Monthly Calendar of the Struggle for Freedom in South Africa," which he signed Optimist, for **Mayibye**, the bulletin of the South African National Congress, printed in Lusaka. Those struggles, incidentally, began as early as 1659, only seven years after the landing of the first Dutch settlers at the Cape. The Khoi-Khoin (commonly called Hottentots), led by Chief Autshumayo, fought hard to prevent Van Reibeeck's seizure of their best pasture land in the Cape Peninsula.

In his introductory paragraph, Alphaeus noted that victory must be won over the forces of tyranny and oppression in South Africa for the people then imprisoned in that police-state, and for their children of tomorrow. "But let us not forget," he said, "that it must also be won for the sake of the countless thousands who, for three hundred years, have suffered and died for the right to live as free men in their native land." As a historian, Alphaeus understood, years ago, that the oppressors of Africans and people of color around the world were one and the same.

Mornings, he spent in the archives or the library and continued his work at home in the afternoon. More often than not, it ran into the evening. Companionship and privacy, aloneness and a current of life around him, again reflected his mood in his frequent desire for me to sit in his study while he worked, and I read. There was no ping-pong to relieve his tension but two-handed bridge was a real tonic. Gradually his healthy appetite began to wane, with a consequent loss of weight, and we decided to go to Livingstone for a week. Perhaps the change would lift his spirit, and exercise give tone to his body. He had grudgingly begun to take morning walks before work, but it was a far cry from what he needed.

To acquire the essence of a country, one must pass beyond the bustling cities. Then, you feel the beauty of the land, as you contemplate its secrets. So much of the land in Zambia is lonely and empty, just waiting for someone to embrace it. Occasionally we saw a hut, almost hidden in the grass, and a village here and there, as we drove by. While traveling through such a countryside, a sense of solitude and hopelessness is hard to push aside while you gaze upon the vast, rich, unused areas.

Livingstone, Zambia's oldest town, is situated at the southern tip of the country. We checked in at the new Inter-Continental Hotel, Musi-o-Tunya, overlooking one of the natural wonders of the world, Victoria Falls. In that refreshing environment, Alphaeus could unbend, swim, enjoy a week of fun, and forget about Africa's problems and his own. Though it was our second visit to the Falls, we felt again a thrill and a sense of awe along with other sightseers clustered on its brink, as we watched that astounding force of unrestrained power plunge 350 feet over the rock face. It tumbles into the first of eight queerly shaped gorges through which the once placid Zambezi River twists before emptying into Lake Kariba some 70 miles away. At the height of the flood waters, when the swift current crashes into the forges with a deadening roar, sending up columns of spray that can be seen 20 miles away, ancient tribesmen called the sight Musi-o-Tunya, "The Smoke That Thunders." Each day we discovered new delights, especially the Look Out Trees where one stood on platforms to command a better view, and a full stretch of the falls.

Alphaeus showed particular interest in the National Museum of Zambia, in the Victoria Falls-Livingstone Complex. It housed a special collection relating to the various tribes, and the life and work of the Scottish missionary-explorer, David Livingstone. Included in the complex is an Open Air Museum with a traditional village established to preserve the ancient arts and crafts of Zambia. Every important event in the life of the village was commemorated by ceremonials, including music and dancing. We spent an entire afternoon observing ritual dances, and watching with astonishment craftsmen who plied their age-old trades, using the same tools and methods employed by their forefathers for centuries.

The trip provided a release for Alphaeus's mind and spirit, and spurred his zest for digging into history. He ate well, slept well, and by the end of the week he felt in good shape. But soon after our return to Lusaka, he complained again of poor digestion. Then began the round of doctors, x-rays and tests. Each doctor gave a different diagnosis.

Many Chinese doctors came to Zambia to attend the thousands of Chinese workers constructing The Great Uhuru Railroad, 1,200 miles long, that will connect Zambia to Tanzania's Indian Ocean port of Dar es Salaam. Though they had no license to practice in Zambia, they treated hundreds of peasants in the bush, without payment. I had been taking acupuncture from Dr. Chin, stationed in Lusaka, and prevailed upon Alphaeus to see him. He concluded there was malfunction of the liver, but he was not in a position to treat him. Alphaeus' condition slowly deteriorated. After some persuasion, he decided to enter London Clinic, but insisted there was no need for me to accompany him to England, much to my annoyance. Yet, several days later, a cable urged me to come at once.

Thanks to Vice-President Simon Kapwepwe, who took care of all the details, my departure went smoothly. Not so my arrival. To add to my anguish, no one had the slightest idea what had happened to my baggage. It was not on the plane. There I stood, shivering in the cold, bleak, November morning, wondering what to do next. A call to the doctor, who directed me to his office, settled that. Alphaeus had already undergone surgery. Somehow I knew the verdict, but I fought against the dreaded thought.

"They opened him up," Dr. Ratner said, "took one look, and closed him up immediately." I no longer fought but cried.

"Shall I tell him?" Dr. Ratner asked, looking directly into my clouded eyes.

"No!" I said. "But you must give him a very good reason for his weakness."

Alphaeus accepted the doctor's explanation, and cooperated in every respect with his usual dignity and graciousness. Little did he know that four or five weeks of life, at most, was all the doctor could predict for him. Cancer of the pancreas, though one of the least painful, is one of the most devastating of all cancers. I marveled at his grit and determination, as did those who served him in the hospital. They were touched by his gentle nature, and great capacity for sympathy and understanding.

We took a room in a small hotel, since Alphaeus' condition prevented travel. Each morning, he braced himself for the short trip to the doctor's office for injections to build his waning energy. It would require his utmost strength of will to withstand the long, tiresome trip to Zambia. He grew increasingly weaker, but fortunately there was little or no pain. A faint shadow of impending death began to appear gradually in the deep, sunken eyes, and the gray pallor of his skin. I was eager to get him to Lusaka before he became completely incapacitated. For one who felt the woes of the underpriviledged as keenly as Alphaeus, and who had committed his life to alleviating those woes, to be out of action and devitalized was especially distressing. The grief and despair that dogged his efforts, and afflicted his soul, finally afflicted his body. But he was unaware of the inevitable consequences of his illness. He had hope.

The flight back wreaked sheer torture. I see-sawed between optimism and panic. Cramped in the narrow seat, with no room for his long legs, Alphaeus shifted and sighed, and seemed in utter misery. A four hour stop-over in Nairobi, Kenya, however, gave him a chance to stretch out in a hotel bed and sleep. When we stopped in Dar es Salaam, Tanazania, the heat created another problem. He was too ill to move. The plane emptied; they turned the air-conditioner off, and I thought surely that was the end. But the stewardess quickly administered oxygen, followed it by a good, stiff brandy, and Alphaeus revived. We finished the trip without further incident.

It was nearly evening when we reached Lusaka. Though he still did not complain, his haggard face portrayed the ruthless force destroying his body. Despite the jaunty angle of his black beret, and his warm, gentle smile of greeting, the Gordons, who met us, were shocked at his features. Barney wheeled him to his car, and home soon came into view.

Knowing his time was short, I refused to put him in the hospital, as the doctor suggested. Each day counted, and must be filled to the utmost with love and peace in the serenity of home. I wanted to be near at all times to minister to his needs. The steward gave him a better shave than I could, but that was the only thing he would allow anyone else to do for him.

He enjoyed sitting by the big, picture window that looked out on the garden. In the comfortable lounge chair a friend gave him, he read newspapers, clipped articles, dozed, and frequently watched me out of the corner of his eye. The third week, while sitting there one day, he asked to see the mirror I had just placed in the drawer. I argued vigorously against it, but he insisted. One look at himself and he exclaimed, "My God! I'm nothing but skin and bones." And so he was. His face was gaunt, but expressive; even a light showed in those searching eyes, though the whites had turned yellow, and a light mist appeared.

He handed me the mirror, looked directly at my strained face, and without a word turned his head towards the garden. Until then, he had had hope. Now he knew. No words came to break the spell. The need to pretend vanished. Yet neither of us could bring ourself to discuss the inescapable.

It was a great mistake. I wanted desperately to talk. Many times, during the last days, I sat beside his bed, and tried to draw him out in the hope that he would raise the subject. But the conspiracy of silence society has thrown around the fact of death had sealed his lips, and to my regret, I did not force the issue.

The night before Alphaeus died, he declined to watch TV, which he had done practically every night. In our absence, a friend had presented it to us to relieve some of his long hours in bed. He felt tired, and so did I. After trying to make him comfortable for the night, I retired to the adjoining bedroom. In the middle of the night I awoke suddenly. Someone had called, "Dorothy!" I bounced out of bed and rushed to Alphaeus, but he was sleeping peacefully. I returned to bed, dozed off, and again leaped up at the sound of my name, this time louder. Alphaeus, still slept soundly. Could I have been dreaming? I doubt it. I catnapped for the rest of the night, and just before dawn, a feeble "Dorothy!" again brought me upright in bed.

When I reached Alphaeus, death sweat had drenched his pajamas, and little pools of water filled the deep hollows around his neck. His unseeing eyes, glossed over and staring straight ahead, remained gentle and kind even in death. I took his cold hand in mine, and held it tight. The hand no longer needed to fold into a fist. Peace at last pervaded his soul.

A withering darkness descended over me. A hopeless sorrow permeated the room, as the great heave of that sympathetic heart grew still, and Alphaeus quietly slipped into another realm. Those lonely acts, birth and death, are painfully private, and incapable of being shared.

Thoughts of a friend, whose letter I had read to Alphaeus just the day before, came to mind. The silence in the room had by now become deafening. She admonished him to keep his courage intact because, "You see my **very** dear friend, the world needs you in this great forward movement of humanity... There is only one Alphaeus Hunton! You have shown heroism in your long, and often difficult life. You must become a hero on the battlefield of illness as well."

Death, be not proud! Alphaeus lost on the battlefield of disease, though he put up a gallant fight. Yet, on the front line of life, he won. His superior intelligence and understanding which enabled him to accept and triumph over misfortune had equipped him to fashion some of the pillars on which young, militant Blacks now stand. This he could not have achieved without a patience that nothing could weary and a devotion of which few men are capable.

There were things to be done without unnecessary waste of time to make his dream of a finer, more just world appear. And in that, his sincere dedication none could challenge. The political arena, as well as the archives, libraries, universities and numerous committees — all those and more were his workshops. Alphaeus never changed. Nor did he ever divorce his beliefs from his actions. Throughout his life, he was essentially himself. The one loyalty that never failed was loyalty to his inner self. He found his strength in his own spirit, and his hopes in the day to come.

The phone had been out of order for several days, but incoming calls came through. I sat beside my beloved and waited, bewildered and stunned.

The shrill ringing of the phone jolted me out of my trance-like consciousness, and I slowly returned to reality. Friends soon came to help. The following day, his body lay in our lovely home, which no longer held any beauty for me. There was no service. That afternoon, Vice-President and Mrs. Simon Kapwepwe, several other high government officials, and a host of friends filled the large living room. Others waited quietly outside. Perhaps an hour passed before President and Mrs. Kenneth Kaunda arrived, after which the long, slow drive to Leopard's Hill Cemetery began.

They tell me the day was hot and clear on January 14, 1970, not a dark cloud in the sky, unusual for the rainy season. Yet I have no recollection of it. I recall only the gravelled walk behind the hearse from the entrance to the grave-site that seemed endless. We passed the Moslem, Hindu, Anglican, and finally came to the Non-Conformist section. There, the dark soil of Alphaeus' forefathers had been moved aside, the better to embrace the scholar-warrior. The obituary, read by the Secretary-General to the Government, Mr. John Mwanakatwe, I had reluctantly started to prepare shortly after we returned from London. Bit by bit had been added as time permitted from my nursing. Only the day before Alphaeus died did I finish it.

The President spoke, standing at the head of the grave beside the Vice-President. He was deeply moved. Midway through the speech he began to weep and seemed unable to continue. Yet, he recovered and completed his tribute to Alphaeus, after which he led the mourners in a hymn as they lowered the coffin. I did not stay to witness that. The ordeal had left me spent, and friends took me home.

Messages came from many friends, at home and abroad. The telegram from the National Council of American Soviet Friendship, signed by Rockwell Kent, National Chairman, William Howard Melish, Board Chairman, and Richard Morford, Director, especially moved me. It read:

> Friends in leadership of the National Council sorrow in the death of Alphaeus. To the cause of international friendship and a peaceful world he gave the fullest measure of devotion. We remember him in service of that cause as a member of our Board of Directors. Your comfort in loneliness now will be the cherished memory of happy companionship in other years, your sense of having been a faithful partner in the resolute efforts to promote freedom, self-appreciation and human dignity of the African people, of giving support in the dark hours of illness. Our

> sympathy extended to you is coupled with a tribute to
> his noble life. His life inspires us to push forward in
> the struggle toward a world of brotherhood.

Another touching letter came from a young girl in college, whom Alphaeus had known as a young child in Brooklyn, and whom he encouraged in her artistic abilities. The news of his death distressed her terribly. She concluded her message: "I am sorry I only knew him from a distance (of age and then geography), but I hope even a small part of his beauty over that distance found its way to me so that I can live as beautifully and honestly as he did."

In May, I returned to New York to start a new life alone. Yet, I was not really alone, for Alphaeus still lives. I often feel his presence, particularly when depression descends and clouds my vision. On September 20, 1970, a day I shall always remember with love, friends filled the United Nations Church Center to overflowing at the memorial service held for Alphaeus. The speakers, introduced by Mrs. Estelle Osborne, paid tribute to many aspects of his full and productive life. After Mr. John Henrik Clarke, Mr. George B. Murphy, Jr., and Dr. Doxey Wilkerson spoke, Miss Nadyne Brewer, accompanied by Mr. Carroll Hollister, sang. Then Mr. William Patterson, Dr. Herbert Aptheker, and the Hon. John Mwanakatwe, Secretary-General to the Zambian government, spoke briefly. Unfortunately, for some strange reason, the message sent by President Kaunda was unduly delayed. It came the following day, and said in part:

> As you gather to commemorate the death of Dr.
> W.A. Hunton, I want you to know that my prayers
> and those of the Party Government and people of
> Zambia are with you. We join you in praying for the
> continued repose of the soul of Dr. Hunton. His ser-
> vices in Zambia are still remembered, and
> cherished. His devotion to the cause of humanity, the
> dignity and worth of the human person regardless of
> color, race, or creed continue to encourage and inspire
> me....

Mr. Vernon J. Mwaanga, Permanent Representative of Zambia to the U.N., relayed the message of the President's deep attachment to Alphaeus, and assured me of his continued personal friendship.

Mr. Mwanakatwe, who was Zambia's first Black Minister of Education for three years, gave a moving speech in which he related how Alphaeus' advice and guidance had helped in the development and consolidation of the Kenneth Kaunda Foundation, and in the transformation of the teaching of literature in his country, whose culture had been badly damaged, in fact, almost destroyed. "He is mourned," he said, "not only by the President and Vice-President, various government ministers, scholars from Zambia's university, and others, but by the entire nation." He deemed it a privilege to speak to those who knew Alphaeus as a friend, a freedom fighter, and comrade in arms. "He is greatly respected in our country," he told the listeners, and "even in death you should have nothing but pride in the work which this man, whom you knew so well, did, not only for Zambia, but for the whole of Africa. A man who endeavored in his own quiet way to show the extent to which the roots run so deep, which connect Blacks of America to the Blacks of Africa."

To me, a fitting and lasting memorial to Alphaeus is not one to be found in a mound of earth and a chiseled stone, but the completion of the **Encyclopedia Africana,** as quickly as possible, that would once and for all dispel the racist myths so blatantly recorded in the annals of history. Alphaeus laid the foundation, and the work cries out for continuation. The respect, the admiration and the intellectual production he elicited from the growing brotherhood of African scholars constitute the basis for renewed action. Let them get on with the job! For, as he wrote in **Mayibue,** June 1968:

Men die, but their ideas and movements live on. We who carry on the struggle today are the heirs of those who went before us. Their strivings, failures and accomplishments must form an integral part of our present consciousness; must enable us to understand more clearly our present task; must fire something within us, making us stronger and better fighters.

Conakry, Guinea, 1962

REFERENCES

CHAPTER 1. THE BEGINNING

1. **William Alphaeus Hunton. A Pioneer Prophet of Young Men** by Addie Waite Hunton. Association Press, New York, 1938, p. 4.
2. Ibid.
3. Ibid.
4. Rev. Jesse E. Moorland letters. Moorland-Spingarn Collection, Founders Library, Howard University.
5. Ibid.
6. Y.M.C.A. Jesse E. Moorland, **Journal of Negro History.** April, 1929, Vol. 9, No. 2, p. 134.
7. **History of Colored Work.** 1907 - 1912. Compiled by Jane Olcott Walters. Nov. - Dec. 1920. Y.W.C.A. Library, N.Y.
8. Ibid.
9. The Brooklyn Eagle Press, New York, 1920.

CHAPTER 2. HOWARD UNIVERSITY

1. **Howard University Annual Catalogue.** 1928-1929.
2. Letter from Dr. Philip Butcher.

CHAPTER 4. THE NATIONAL NEGRO CONGRESS

1. "William Alphaeus Hunton: A Life that Made a Difference" by Dr. Doxey Wilkerson. **Freedomways** Vol. 10, No. 3, Third Quarter 1970.

CHAPTER 9. GUINEA

1. **Africa. The National Geographic.** Vol. 118, No. 3, September 1960. p. 305
2. "Opening Address to the 2nd National J.D.R.A. Congress in Conakry."
3. "Freetown, Tropical Africa". Life World Library, p.126
4. "Great Ages of Man," **African Kingdoms,** by Basil Davidson, Time Inc. 1970
5. **Decision in Africa,** p. 30.

CHAPTER 10. THE ENCYCLOPEDIA AFRICANA

1. "The Last Days of Dr. Du Bois — African Patriot," by Alphaeus Hunton. **National Guardian,** February 18, 1967.
2. **Dark Days in Africa** by Kwame Nkrumah, p. 54.
3. **Aggrey of Africa** by Edwin W. Smith, p. 227. Richard R. Smith, Inc. New York 1930.
4. Ibid. p.224.
5. **Dark Days in Africa,** Kwame Nkrumah, p. 41.

CHAPTER 11. SHATTERED HOPES

1. **Dark Days in Africa,** Kwame Nkrumah, p. 49.

APPENDIX

LIST OF WRITINGS BY ALPHAEUS HUNTON

Books:

Tennyson and the Victorian Political Milieu. Abridgment of thesis. New York University, 1938.
William Morris, The Craftsman; William Morris, The Man.
The Ivory Tower of the Victorians.
Some Adverse Criticism of Arnold by His Contemporaries.
Decision in Africa. International Publishers, 1957, 1960.

Pamphlets: Council on African Affairs:

Stop South Africa's Crimes. 1946
Resistance Against Facist Enslavement in South Africa. 1953
Seeing Is Believing - The Truth About South Africa. 1947
Africa Fights for Freedom. 1950
Bandung; Asian-African Conference. April 1955
Review of the Asian-African Conference. May 1955
American Labor and the Future of the African Workers.

Magazine Articles:

"Shall We Affiliate." **American Teacher,** 1938.
"A Teacher's Creed." **Howard Teacher's Union Bulletin,** 1941
"For Fundamental Freedom for All" **Soviet Union Today,** Nov. 1950.
    Summerized in **Freedom,** November 1950
"Eboue: A Man to Remember." **New Masses,** September 12, 1944.
"West Africa Today." **Political Affairs,** 1959.
"Upsurge in Africa." **Masses and Mainstreams,** February 1950
"Central Africa and Freedom." **Political Affairs,** April 1959.
"A Letter from Guinea." **Political Affairs,** August 1960
"Africa's Hidden Past," a review of **The Lost Cities of Africa**
    by Basil Davidson. **New World Review,** 1960.
"Africa and Neo-Colonailism." **Political Affairs,** February 1961.
"Guinea Strides Forward." First issue of **Freedomways,** 1961.
    Also in **Fighting Back,** November 1961.
"Richard Wright." **Europe - revue mensuelle,** France, Juin 1962
"W.E.B. Du Bois: The Meaning of His Life." **Freedomways,** Fall 1963.
"Concerning the **Encyclopedia Africana.**" **Freedomways,** Fall 1967.
"Africa: Operation Jackpot." **Masses and Mainstream.**
"A Monthly Calendar of the Struggle for Freedom in South Africa."
    Mayibuye, June 1968 - February 1969.

Newspaper Articles:

"Nigerians Fight for a Living Wage." The Peoples Voice,
    August 11, 1945.
"Answer Now, General Smuts." **The Peoples Voice,**
September 7, 1946
"Hush-Hush at Lake Success." **The Worker,** October 19, 1947
"The Meaning of Dr. Du Bois' Life." **The Ghanaian Times,**
    September 5, 1963.
"The Present Is Child of the Past." **The Spark,** Ghana, April 5, 1963
    (Chapter 1 in **Decision in Africa.**)
"The Last Years of Dr. Du Bois' Life - African Patriot." **The National
    Guardian,** February 18, 1967.

Addresses on Africa, etc.:

"Problems of Negroes in Our Society." Teachers Union Conference, Chicago, 1938.

"The Past and Future of the Y.M.C.A. Among Negroes." National Laymen's Conference, Bordentown, N.J., July 16, 1944.

"Africa, A Continent in Bondage to Imperialism." Fellowship for a Christian Social Order, Toronto, March 1944.

"The Stakes for Peace and Freedom in Africa."

"Facts about the Union of South Africa: South Africa's Aggressive Imperialism." May 1946

"Testimony: In Opposition to the North Atlantic Treaty." Hearing of the Senate Foreign Relations Committee, Washington, D.C., May 13, 1949.

"American Trusts Bolster South African Racists." 1951.

"Liberia's Exploiters Hail Tubman's Inauguration." February 1952.

"State Department Winks at Malan's Church Ban." April 1953.

"South Africans Organize Congress of the People." January 1955.

"U.S. Upholds Shame of Oppression in South Africa." March 1955.

"Some Problems of African Liberation in White Settler Countries." 1959.

"Postscripts on Nkrumah's Visit."

"On the Question of African Neutralism." U.S.S.R., 1961.

"Present Task of the African Liberation Struggle and the Role of the U.S." Hungary, 1961.

"Let the African People Speak."

"The Present State of the African Liberation Struggle." East Germany, 1961.

"The Stakes of Peace and Freedom in Africa." "The Roots of Pan-Africanism." Kumasi, Ghana, September 16, 1963.

"The Role of the **Encyclopedia Africana** in Understanding the New Africa." The Sixteenth Annual New Year School, University of Ghana, January 3, 1965.

"What Dr. Du Bois Gave Humanity." Ghana.

176

Printed by Eppress Speed Print, Inc.
1625 Amsterdam Avenue, New York, New York 10031

www.ingramcontent.com/pod-product-compliance
Lightning Source LLC
Chambersburg PA
CBHW071953090426
42740CB00011B/1920